12.95
W9-AHK-372

LIVING, LOVING, LEADING

LIVING, LOVING, LEADING

Creating a home that encourages spiritual growth

David & Karen Mains

10209 SE Division Street, Portland, Oregon 97266

Scripture references are from the Holy Bible: New International Version, copyright 1973, 1978, 1984, by the International Bible Society. Used by permission of Zondervan Bible Publishers.
Scripture references marked NKJV are from the Holy Bible: New King James Version © 1982, 1984 by Thomas Nelson, Inc.

Edited by Steve Halliday
Cover design by Bruce DeRoos

LIVING, LOVING, LEADING
© 1988 David and Karen Mains
Published by Multnomah Press
Portland, Oregon 97266

Multnomah Press is a ministry of Multnomah School of the Bible,
8435 Northeast Glisan Street, Portland, Oregon 97220

Printed in the United States of America

All rights reserved. No part of this publication may be reproduced, stored in a retrieval system, or transmitted, in any form or by any means, electronic, mechanical, photocopying, recording, or otherwise, without the prior written permission of the publisher.

Library of Congress Cataloging-in-Publication Data

Mains, David R.
Living, loving, leading / David and Karen Mains.
p. cm.
Included Bibliographies.
ISBN 0-88070-225-7
1. Family—Religious life. 2. Marriage—Religious aspects-
-Christianity. 3. Mains, David R. 4. Mains, Karen Burton.
I. Mains, Karen Burton. II. Title.
BV4526.2.M25 1988
248.4—dc19 88-39101
CIP

89 90 91 92 93 94 95 96 97 - 10 9 8 7 6 5 4 3 2

To Valerie Briggs and Jack Risley,
loving burden-bearers,
who believe in celebrations.

Contents

Part Two: Making It Work as Families

Prologue

A young wife, perplexed and visibly frustrated, asked, "How do I get my husband to be the spiritual head of the family?"

The question poses an interesting conundrum: How does the follower get the leader to be the leader so that the follower can stop leading and let the leader lead the follower?

Women who ask this question often presuppose that their husbands are not interested in spiritual leadership—and it is true that some men are not. It is our firm conviction, however, that most Christian husbands *are* concerned. They just get stuck in one of many traps:

- They don't have models that fit their contemporary marriage situation.
- They don't have appropriate forums in which they can interact with and adapt ideas based on careful biblical study.
- They have seen one form of leadership presented as *the* spiritual way—and have found

that this way inadequately matches their unique, individual styles.

The truth is, spiritual leadership in the Christian home is a puzzle to a significant number of couples these days. A host of theological, sociological, and cultural reasons contribute to this contemporary marital malaise, and the end result is confusion.

Opinions regarding spiritual leadership in the home are almost endless. Some cling to the idea that the man is the "head," and by this mean that he makes all the decisions; his word is final. We heard this opinion expressed recently at a banquet table by a group of wives whose husbands work at a large church. One woman mentioned that she left all the decision-making up to her husband, and the others quickly agreed: "That's what the Bible teaches!"

Other couples believe that an egalitarian arrangement with mutuality in decision-making is best for them, and that "headship" in Scripture really doesn't mean what some have taught it to mean, *i.e.* that the husband is over the wife in a hierarchical chain of command. Instead, they believe he is an enabler, a servant who brings to completion all God desires for his wife to be.

So who's right? Who's wrong? And what to do now?

We are extremely sensitive to these issues because this Mains marriage has been forged in that generation struggling to cope with the seismic shifts occurring in the earth plates of men-women relationships since World War II. For three decades now, our personal husband/wife relationship has been a practical laboratory in which to test the scriptural truths which we hold dear—in spite of the quakes imposed by the challenges of modern culture.

We believe we have implemented spiritual principles which not only have served us well but which can be applied to the wide range of views held about spiritual

The New Reality

Confusion over the meaning of spiritual leadership in the home is caused partly by a great shift in our society. Male and female roles are being redefined; the nuclear family has come under focused attack; the economics of the working place are rapidly changing both attitudes and lifestyles.

Recent statistics suggest that the full-time homemaker is now "obsolete" because of economic pressures. At the beginning of the 1980s, well over forty million American women were working for pay—about 50 percent of the civilian labor force. Women are swelling the work force at the rate of almost two million every year. Eli Ginzberg, former head of the National Commission for Manpower Policy, stated, "It changes the relationship of men to women; it changes the relationship of mothers to children. And the future of the suburbs may also be in doubt."

A study by the Urban Institute suggests that in the 1990s three-fourths of all married men and two-thirds of all mothers will hold jobs. Not only are women working, they are working longer, joining the work force for 22.9 years as opposed to twelve years in 1940. The 1981 Census Bureau showed that 49.8 percent of all bachelor's degrees awarded that year were earned by women. Seventy percent of all college-educated women work. Virtually all women in their twenties and thirties work unless they have small children, and even then, half the women with children under six work. Some forecasters estimate that women's participation in the labor force will soon approach that of men, at 75 percent.[1]

1. Karen Mains, "It's a Puzzle to Me," *Christianity Today*, July 17, 1981, p. 57.

leadership in Christian families. We also believe one of the most important discussions of our age is that of male/ female roles and functions. Consequently, we believe that what we have to share is of extreme urgency.

This is not a typical "how-to." We will not develop a rigid plan for becoming a spiritual leader, as if only one were legitimate. We are convinced that particular couples will develop their own particular styles. The specific style is not important—the creation of a Christ-centered home is.

We will describe what such a home offers, discuss the contemporary challenges to developing it, and try to candidly share our own struggles and triumphs.

Many of you will want to know a little about us and about the foundational ideas which shape this book. From what position are David and Karen Mains thinking through the idea of spiritual leadership in the home?

Two important concepts help guide our thoughts on this subject. We'll look at each in greater detail later on, but for now let us give you a thumbnail sketch of our perspective.

First, we believe that when Scripture teaches that the male is the head of the family, it means (primarily) that the father or husband is responsible before God to ensure that his family enjoys an environment of healthy spirituality. Too often arguments about male headship center on decision-making, authority, or hierarchy, and thus miss the critical issue.

Frankly, we believe it is more important to answer the question, "Is this Christian family growing spiritually?" and "Who will ultimately be responsible before God if this unit fails in that unique mandate?" than to ask, "Who gets the last word?"

Second, our own marriage is based on a concept we call "The Marriage Executive Team." The husband, as the head, elevates his wife to a position of co-regency. While remaining the "head," he does everything in his power to help his mate become all that God meant her to be. Husband and wife together guide and direct their household as equal partners, each spouse discovering and using whatever unique talents God has given them.

In trying to model these concepts we have presented our ideas in several ways. Karen has written some chapters, David others. Dialogues between ourselves are included which try to show how differing perspectives can work together to forge effective strategies. Study questions are included to help readers, both as individuals and as couples, design effective "how-to-do-its" appropriate to households of many kinds.

This book is not so much an architect's blueprint for building a spiritually-sensitive home as it is an artist's preliminary sketch of a proposed sculpture. The basic outlines are there, but different craftspeople will fashion and shape that sculpture in ways appropriate to their own talents and abilities.

Before we go any further, we think you might want to know who it is who has dared to take pen in hand to offer counsel on a subject as delicate as spiritual leadership in the home. Who are David and Karen Mains, and what qualifies us to write such a book?

Who Are We?

We often think of ourselves as a kind of Christian Laurel and Hardy. "Oh-ho-ho," God must laugh. "There go the Mainses again; time for some comic relief."

Why the laughter? To begin with, we are almost exact opposites.

According to the Myers-Briggs Type Indicator—a character and temperament analysis test included and amplified in the book *Please Understand Me* by David Keirsey and Marilyn Bates—we are the classic attracting opposites.

Without going into the test in detail, let us say that David is an *extrovert* (E) while Karen is an *introvert* (I). We are both *intuitives* (N). David filters the world through a *thinking* (T) mode, while Karen filters that same world through a *feeling* (F) mode. Finally, David formulates conclusions decisively; he makes decisions by *judging* and therefore is a (J). Karen prefers to leave all her options open for as long as possible, *perceiving* all data, and is therefore a (P).

The sum total of our individual types make David an an ENTJ and Karen an INFP. David's code name is Field Marshal. He loves to command "armies" with an eye to long-term strategies and their derivative tactics, logistics, and consequences. Karen's code name is Questor, a kind of modern Joan of Arc, a contemplative drawn to the inner world of prayer and solitude as well as an occasional crusader given to causes and salvaging operations.

These differences can best be seen by the way we prefer to go on vacations.

David loves to have the road, the finances, the hotels, the events mapped out weeks ahead of time. Chart it. Plan it. Control it. Coordinate it.

Karen prefers simply to get in the car, point it in a certain direction, and follow the road. She loves to chase rabbit tracks, stop at antique shops and roadside vegetable stands, meander through country fairs. She doesn't want to know where she's going; she just wants to find out where she's arrived after she's gotten there!

"There's a lot of danger in that," says David. "You might have a disastrous couple of days. Your non-plans might fail."

"That's true," Karen replies, "but think of the surprises you might encounter! Think of the adventure, the unknown people you might meet!"

Actually, until just recently, all the Mains's vacations were done according to the ENTJ design. But a few years ago, after saving money for quite a while, we took a two-week dream vacation to England—one of the rare vacations without ministry obligations, without a week of speaking to pay for the travel, without any plans, without having to be in any place at any set time for any reason. It was wonderful!

David had his doubts, but he was trying to prove to Karen that he could do it her way. So we bought into one of those economy hotel plans in which all you have to do is call ahead one day in advance.

And the first day—the first day!—we set off in our rented car for once in our marriage without a master vacation plan. We followed the open road, turned off the highway to Dover Castle and just happened—just happened!—to hit it on the very day of a medieval festival. Jousting, revelry, broadsword fighting on the greens, cannon salutes to the queen, longbow archery demonstrations. That afternoon, we sauntered into Canterbury, to the cathedral, and happened—just happened—upon a reunion of several hundred veterans of the Normandy invasion.

Hundreds of these old men were preparing to march through the streets of the town. They had come from all over England, former soldiers who had survived the slaughter on the beaches at Normandy forty-four years earlier. We watched as they gathered behind banners. Drummers began to beat and the men slowly moved out, some limping. At curbside, their wives waved and cheered them on, singing "It's a Long Way to Tipperary."

What an emotional moment, this little slice of history we stumbled upon while doing our anniversary vacation

Karen's way! Then we "just happened" to walk into Canterbury Cathedral at the very moment evensong was being sung in the choir.

"A perfect day!" Karen crowed. "An absolutely perfect, unplanned day!"

"It rained the whole time we were in England," David recalled.

But that didn't matter. The memories linger of the Cotswolds, Stratford-upon-Avon, learning to take the tube (the subway) in London, the London Museum . . .

Of course, there *was* one moment of panic about midway in our unplanned vacation. We were in Oxford and Karen couldn't find rooms for the next few nights. All our economy hotels were filled. Karen had made at least fifteen phone calls. No room in any inn.

And David made one call . . .

"Not fair!" Karen says. "David had an ancillary list of hotels that I didn't know about."

"Just in case, just in case," David says. And he did find lodging.

The only day it didn't rain was on our anniversary. We grabbed the moment, walking through Regents Park and its acres of roses in bloom. We sat on plastic sacks on the damp grass in the welcome sunshine, watching and laughing at an outdoor performance of Shakespeare's *A Midsummer Night's Dream*. We even got tickets—first balcony, front row center—to *Les Misérables*, the smash musical that had been sold out for four months. Someone turned them in at exactly the moment David stepped to the box office window. A gift of God!

David admits today that doing it Karen's way was a lot of fun. The panic in Oxford, he thinks, was thrown in just to salvage his wounded pride.

But note that it took this Laurel-and-Hardy team twenty-six years to get around to Karen's way!

We frequently quote a line from the play, *Man of La Mancha*. Sancho Panza, Don Quixote's roly-poly sidekick, cries, "Off to more misadventure!" A hallmark of our married life together is that we take on projects that have great failure potential.

When we were first married, David was a Youth for Christ rally director. And at a brave nineteen years of age, Karen decided that she could prepare the meal at a fund-raiser for two hundred donors. True, she'd never tackled a turkey dinner before; but what she lacked in experience she made up for in enormous self-confidence!

Unfortunately, she hadn't counted on *frozen* turkeys. So when David came home the night before the dinner to his newlywed apartment—hot, tired and sweaty, longing for a shower—he was unprepared to discover four denuded, headless carcasses floating in the bathtub!

We can't remember if he ever got his shower. But it seems that there have always been a lot of frozen turkey carcasses inconveniently floating around in our marital lives.

Starting a church in the inner city was one. We dreamed and planned and pulled together a little band of people committed to the vision of making a contemporary church into what God intended his church to be.

It took a year and a half of planning, praying, philosophizing, and theologizing. After much prayer, David found a Teamster's union hall across from the Circle Interchange, met with Louis Peick, the head of Local 705, and told him that we believed God wanted us to start a church in the inner city. From the first meeting, Mr. Peick always called David "Reverend." "What this city needs is another God-damned Protestant church!" he said, and gave us the former plasterer's union dance hall in which to meet Sunday after Sunday. For ten years we met in that union hall, rent-free.

Our first Sunday service began in the midst of one of Chicago's worst snowfalls and attracted only twenty-seven faithful, weather-brave souls. But that little church grew into Circle Church, a robust, thriving commuter church of some five hundred. People came from all over the city, a lot of 1970s types: some barefoot, long-haired, beaded hippies giving church one last try; all young, anti-authoritarian, bright, creative. International students. Blacks. We had an inter-racial staff, an inter-racial congregation. We thought we knew everything.

And learned that we didn't. One day the church split along racial lines.

That was a failure, and it hurt. We failed in front of all those across the nation who were keeping an eye on our efforts. We failed in front of all those who said the most successful church is homogeneous, alike. We had insisted that the body of Christ is heterogeneous, broad, different, racially diverse, economically stratified. We believed that the commonality of the Holy Spirit would bind us together . . . and discovered that, whereas that might be ideally true, humanly we weren't strong enough to make it happen.

And so, after ten years of constant ecclesiastical experiment, we left to take up the reins of "The Chapel of the Air," one of the first religious broadcasts to start soon after the airwaves were cleared by the Federal Communications Commission for religious programming late in the 1930s.

Again, experts said it couldn't be done. It would be next to impossible, they said, to transition a broadcast from a single voice (that of John D. Jess) to a multiple team sound (husband-and-wife dialogue, interviews), with David's voice as the anchor. But we persisted. On to more misadventure! Plenty of room for pratfalls on a grand scale here!

The first year we offered a program for accelerated spiritual growth; seven thousand individuals signed up. We were thrilled! Since then, our "Fifty Day Spiritual Adventure," offered each spring, has involved over three hundred thousand adventurers, thousands of churches, and untold results in terms of spiritual growth.

But still we struggle.

Raising the finances for a ministry dedicated to issuing a call for national spiritual regenesis has turned David gray, is the deepest burden of our lives, and often makes us feel as though we should find other vocations. The other day, David returned from meetings on the road and said, "Well, I know our ministry touches lives deeply. People testify to me of profound spiritual change. It just doesn't touch *enough* lives."

That is what life has been like for this comedy team of Mains and Mains. And in the midst of all this ministry, in the midst of rearing four children, and while facing hard things—the premature death of parents, endless work, a house that always provides a home for others (we can only think of one year in the last fifteen that we haven't had someone living with us)—we have kept this marriage.

Our personal differences are numerous enough that they could have torn our marriage to pieces. We strongly believe we have as many reasons for divorce as other marriages that do fall apart, but we have learned to make these differences work for us.

Oh, there has been pain. There has been misunderstanding. In fact, making this marriage good is so much work that if anything ever happened to either one of us, the other would have to think twice before remarrying. Could we justify the time and energy subtracted from the work of the Kingdom that a new marriage would require?

Our marriage has become a laboratory for ideas, for

growth, for gentle (and sometimes not-so-gentle) prodding to become all that God intends for us to be.

We are well aware that this is not a perfect union! But with God's help, it has become a productive union, and we believe that our Lord is honored at least by our faithful intent to serve him with our whole hearts.

What has held this marriage together is the common purpose to which we have committed our lives and beings: to advance the cause of Christ and his Kingdom.

Our spiritual life is what has salvaged us. The dedication to work through, around, over, between, above, and behind the differences has come from one cause, and that cause is our commitment to Christ. We have been determined to make this marriage work because of Christ and for his glory, and it has worked to the point where both of us would testify that we couldn't have made it without each other. Through these years, our differences have become utterly complementary.

And that is who we are: Two rather funny people, willing to take risks, who, because of our bottom-line spiritual commitment and the profound effect that spiritual commitment has had on our personal lives, are making a marriage work despite enormous differences. That, above anything else, is what we have to give to other couples.

It is our keen hope that the ideas and counsel in these pages will help your home to grow into a spiritual environment in which husband, wife, and any offspring can learn to love God and serve him.

None of it will be easy. We don't promise you a life free from pratfalls, that you won't sometimes get egg on your faces. There will be moments when all the effort of making marriage work will seem worthless.

Just keep at it. Persevere. You're doing more than forging a comedy team; you, together, are creating a habitation in which Christ himself will be pleased to dwell. You are laboring to construct a home where from time to time you'll catch glimpses of that perfect place, that perfect time, that perfect union of the Lamb and the Bride for which all our hearts deeply long.

And when those moments come, when the supernatural intermingles with the natural, you will be assured that the heavenly home is real and more tangible than we know—a home still future, yet sensed dramatically even now between the two of you, man/woman, husband/wife.

Believe us, that is worth all the effort.

Couples' Discussion Questions

"I wish my husband would be the spiritual head of our home," says a sincere young woman. Yet she interrupts her husband's comments in the small group Bible study. She derides his ideas about scriptural topics. She complains about his handling of the children (or finances, job-planning, recreational activities, etc.). She seems to be subconsciously jettisoning everything she says she wants.

Have you ever been acquainted with such a woman?

Something is going on internally in her which needs honest and forthright appraisal. It may be that her husband really *isn't* fulfilling his biblical responsibilities; but could it also be that he simply doesn't meet her strongly-held, unstated expectations? Is it possible that she has one idea of spiritual headship, while he holds to another?

Married people often live with undiscussed expectations of each other—some unrecognized even by the one who holds them. When these expectations go unfulfilled, disappointment, defeat and failure in communication soon follow. Often these unstated desires are unrealistic, sometimes extra-biblical, and frequently dehumanizing. They are often based on the internal imprint we carry with us that is part of our past family system: "Dad and Mom related to our family like this. Why can't you do it like them?"

At other times these strong desires spring from our own love deprivations, and they can become almost obsessional: "Death and divorce broke my family unit, so I expect you to fill the hole left when my parents failed to meet my emotional needs." Or perhaps they're expectations formed by a skewed culture: "The profile of my economically privileged, upwardly-mobile family with two working professional parents is much better than that of your lower-class, laboring father and home-bound mother."

No area is more fraught with dangerous expectations than that of male spiritual leadership in the Christian family. Before you go any farther in the reading of this book, take a few moments to complete the following self-examination (duplicate questions for both husband and wife are included). After you have finished the book, return to these pages and consider them again in light of the information in and discussions stimulated by *Living, Loving, Leading*.

* * * *

What Do I Mean by Spiritual Headship?
(Husband's copy)

1. Choose three words to describe what you think spiritual leadership in the Christian family should be:

____

2. My mother respected my father's spiritual leadership: Yes or no (circle one). How did she show this?

____

____

3. My father demonstrated that he was a spiritual leader in our family by ______________________________

____

4. In his spiritual leadership, I wish my father had ____

____

5. The ideal spiritual climate in our own Christian family would look like this: ______________________________

____

____

6. My wife could demonstrate lively spirituality by ____

______________________________.

7. My wife encourages my spirituality by ____.

8. The spiritual climate in my own family was________ Why? ______________________________.

9. In regard to the spiritual growth of our family, I am disappointed when my wife __________________. ____

10. I think my own spiritual growth influences my wife to ____ ____

11. I am ______________________ by the spiritual life in our own home.

12. Spirituality becomes tangible when we see one another ____.

13. I would grow more spiritually if ____.

14. A father who leads his family spiritually does these activities: ____ ____.

15. A wife who encourages her husband's spiritual leadership shows it by ____.

16. When my children are grown, I want them to remember these specific acts of spiritual activity: ____ ____.

17. When I am old and my children are adults, I want to be able to say that we trained our children spiritually by ____

____.

18. In regard to spirituality in the Christian family, I think God expects ____________________________

____.

19. My model of spiritual leadership is ____________

20. Our chances as a couple of attaining to my expectation of spirituality in our home are ____________

____

____.

*　*　*　*

What Do I Mean by Spiritual Headship?
(Wife's copy)

1. Choose three words to describe what you think spiritual leadership in the Christian family should be:

____

2. My mother respected my father's spiritual leadership: Yes or no (circle one). How did she show this?

____

____

3. My father demonstrated that he was a spiritual leader in our family by ____________________________

____

4. In his spiritual leadership, I wish my father had ____

____

5. The ideal spiritual climate in our own Christian family would look like this: ____

6. My husband could demonstrate lively spirituality by __________________________________.

7. My husband encourages my spirituality by __________________________________.

8. The spiritual climate in my own family was________ Why? ____________________________.

9. In regard to the spiritual growth of our family, I am disappointed when my husband ______________. __________________________________

10. I think my own spiritual growth influences my husband to ____

11. I am ________________________ by the spiritual life in our own home.

12. Spirituality becomes tangible when we see one another ____.

13. I would grow more spiritually if __________________________________.

14. A father who leads his family spiritually does these activities: ____.

15. A wife who encourages her husband's spiritual leadership shows it by ____.

16. When my children are grown, I want them to remember these specific acts of spiritual activity: ____
____
____.

17. When I am old and my children are adults, I want to be able to say that we trained our children spiritually by ____
____
____.

18. In regard to spirituality in the Christian family, I think God expects ____
____.

19. My model of spiritual leadership is ____________

20. Our chances as a couple of attaining to my expectation of spirituality in our home are ____________
____
____.

Part One

Making It Work as Couples

1 Who's In Charge Here?

David

Most men are willing to work long hours for that next promotion: job boss, head of the department, floor manager, account executive, junior vice president. Job advancement brings headaches, but few men refuse promotions. Pay raises, status, and the opportunity of a new challenge far outweigh any negatives.

Even the words "From now on, you're responsible to see that this project gets done" sound like an opportunity rather than a threat. A promotion means that someone with authority has finally asked, "How would you like to be in charge here?"

But while most men rise to the challenge of job advancement, many seem strangely defeated at the thought of spiritual management in the family.

Scriptural references to headship are found most in the writings of Paul. The apostle uses headship to mean supremacy when referring to Christ. For example, Ephesians 1:22 reads, "And God placed all things under his feet and appointed him [Christ] to be head over everything . . . "

The difficulty in interpreting related passages arises when the same word refers to a husband's relationship to his wife. Ephesians 5:23, 24 read, "For the husband is the head of the wife as Christ is the head of the church . . . as the church submits to Christ, so also wives should submit to their husbands in everything."

The same idea is recorded in 1 Corinthians 11:3: "Now I want you to realize that the head of every man is Christ, and the head of the woman is man . . . " This lends ego gratification to the male if he gives headship the supremacy meaning. Yet few of us, knowing even a little about the nature of Christ, would hold that our Lord viewed the male sex to be supreme.

Lording it over others was not Jesus' style. In no way could you detect in his relationship with women an attitude of male supremacy. Jesus' supremacy stems from his divine nature, from his being the Christ, not from his sex.

The Scriptures do state that wives are to show husbands respect, but Christlike husbands are never free to act like Napoléons. In fact, it was one of that general's soldiers who inspired the term "chauvinism." Nicolas Chauvin was so notorious for his bellicose attachment to the lost Napoleonic imperial cause that his name was given to any unreasoning devotion to one's country, race, or sex.

Male chauvinism and biblical headship are galaxies apart. The first is anti-Christ, the second is Christlike.

Our difficulty with headship stems partially from the fact that its meaning is more implicit in these texts than explicit. In other words, there is no biblical statement that reads, "Headship is definitively to be understood as (1) . . . and (2) . . . etc." Because of this, we run the danger of imposing upon the Bible our own unique styles of leadership and our own favorite variety of authority.

So What's The Problem?

Recently we organized a focus group with younger couples to discuss spiritual leadership in the Christian home. A variety of personal issues were raised. The following comments were made by husbands and give a fair sampling of what many others feel about the subject:

"The changing role of women in our culture has disoriented males as to the meaning of leadership in the home."

"Expectations that many wives have for their husbands are often vague and unarticulated, and sometimes not really understood by the women themselves."

"Women take more spiritual initiative; men are focused on their professions."

"Leadership is not just an issue in the home. We live in an anti-authoritarian culture—witness the character assassination of the last few presidents. We just have a culture of bad followers."

"I've heard hundreds of sermons preached to women on submission, but I've hardly heard any preached to men on what spiritual leadership really is."

"I don't want to make all the decisions. I don't believe in the old authoritarian model. I need my wife to be my fellow companion on this road of life. I need her help to give me self-definition."

The vigor and emotional engagement of the men in this discussion hardly indicated disinterest in the topic of spiritual leadership. These men were intensely interested; they just didn't know how to proceed.

In one church where I pastored, the elders spent several years attempting to define the role of women in the church. After many frustrating discussions, I began to suspect that each elder was defining women's roles according to his own preferred marriage style. One man would say a woman could be involved in a broad range of duties within the church (particularly if his marriage was egalitarian in style) while another would say she should function within a limited scope (particularly if his marriage was traditional and role-oriented in form). Of course, each elder believed his own interpretation was more scriptural than any other interpretation!

In reality, the roles that husband and wife play in a marriage seem to be more a matter of agreement between married partners—a matter of intricately meshing personalities, a matter of preference in lifestyles, a matter of cultural and economic considerations—than it is a matter of biblical precept. Unfortunately, we often argue over forms which are really extra-biblical, and these arguments serve as smoke screens to keep us from understanding the real issue of spiritual headship. Consequently, when I work with small groups of men or in marital counseling situations, I attempt to focus first on the responsibility inherent in leadership, as opposed to the roles of the sexes.

Headship means that the husband assumes ultimate responsibility for the spiritual well-being of his family. In other words, the husband/father is to see to it that the atmosphere of the home is conducive to spiritual health. He is alert, watchful to protect his family from unnecessary evil. He stimulates communication on spiritual matters and fosters the involvement of his family in church.

He does not need to do all the spiritual training, but like the businessman who has just received a promotion, it's his job to see that the task is successfully completed. He has been told, "From now on, you're the one in charge here." Headship can be thought of as being ultimately responsible for the spiritual climate of his department, the family.

Unfortunately, many Christian men like the honor that goes along with headship, but are unenthused about the job description. Many have no concept of how to define spirituality or spiritual authority, and they have few models that demonstrate how to be the head of a family—particularly in light of the complexities of contemporary male/female roles.

Personally, when I begin to wonder about the quality of my own headship, I simply check the kind of spiritual example I am setting in my home.

I once asked participants in a seminar called "Helping Your Children to Grow Spiritually" to think of ways their parents had taught them significant truths. At least 95 percent of them indicated they had learned the most, both positively and negatively, through their parents' examples.

In business, hundreds of thousands of dollars are spent on executive training, management seminars and sales conferences. The adequate preparation of the person who must do the task is essential in order to get the task done.

The same is true with the male who must become the spiritual head. His example, what he models, who he is spiritually, is nine-tenths of the job. Yet there is no credentials committee to conduct an accrediting review of his spiritual headship abilities. There is no management team of consultants who will evaluate strong and weak points. So the Christian husband/father will have to undertake his own spiritual self-examination.

We all need to set time aside and ask:

1. What kind of example am I as the spiritual head of my family?

2. What is good about my headship? What needs to improve?
3. Am I a praying man?
4. Do I really love God's Word?
5. How much time do I give to each of these activities? Do I dare to log my time to keep myself honest?
6. Am I Christlike in overcoming temptations?
7. Do I keep my conscience sensitive to the promptings of the Holy Spirit?
8. Is church life important to me, and do I demonstrate respect for my spiritual leaders?

These questions are enough for a start. After you have asked them of yourself, call your management team (you and your wife) together. Ask her to evaluate where you are on this matter of spiritual headship. Ask her to answer the foregoing questions as an evaluation of your spiritual strengths and weaknesses.

Karen and I regularly evaluate the quality of our marriage as well as the spiritual development of our family. Evaluation sessions are absolutely essential for healthy marriages. It is here that we delegate assignments, pick up responsibilities for one another, hold one another accountable, encourage each other, and tie together loose ends.

In other words, I exercise my spiritual headship by inviting my wife to work alongside me to develop the spiritual climate of our home. Through the years we have become a team, co-workers in this area. She assists me by helping me grow into my full potential as a healthy, spiritual adult. I do the same for her.

Socrates once said, "The unexamined life is not worth living." The problem with most Christian men is that they never examine the fine details of their spiritual headship to discover where and how they can improve.

They just go on feeling guilty that they aren't what they should be. That is a life that is not worth living!

Spiritual headship begins first with the quality of our spiritual examples. I believe the spiritual example of the husband/father in the home will be much more powerful than even the family devotions he attempts to hold or the scripture verses he expects his children to memorize.

The second step in our spiritual headship is in enabling our wives to become 100 percent of what God wants them to be. This again puts us back to the executive question: "Honey, what can I do that will help you become what you feel God wants you to be?" Be concerned about how she is doing with the basics. Are there ways you can encourage her?

Be careful not to point a judgmental finger at her failings, but lovingly invite her to analyze where her spiritual dreams are, where she thinks she can best function and how she can get there. Again, think of Christ saying, "I'm giving you the primary responsibility for the spiritual well-being of your family." All you are doing is talking through this assignment as it relates to your most important co-worker. So what if she is more expert in this department than you are?

The well-known industrialist Andrew Carnegie was asked about the secret of his success. "I always hire men smarter than myself," he replied.

A lot of men have employees who are stronger in certain areas than they are themselves. Be friends with your wife and work together on your spiritual "becoming." Be glad for her strengths. She will make you look good! Remember that she is your greatest asset in this job promotion from God. And the most wonderful truth is that even if she is a saintly giant, she will still be thrilled if you pick up the obligations and responsibilities of spiritual headship.

The two most important ingredients to exercising spiritual headship are a functioning spiritual head and a functioning spiritual co-head. Set aside time when you two family executives talk exclusively about how you both are doing spiritually. Put it on your calendar. Add more times as you need them. There is tremendous strength in a spiritual team working in concert.

The options for the exercise of spiritual headship are endless. They are wonderfully challenging, but not so difficult as they at first seemed.

A question needs to be answered by Christian husbands and fathers. Someone very important has asked, "How would you like to be in charge here?"

My advice is: Take the job!

Couples' Discussion Questions

Studies have discovered that while leadership can be developed, it cannot be taught in a classroom. We learn it by seeing it modeled. Edmund Burke once said, "Example is the school of mankind and they will learn at no other." Consequently, if fewer leaders are trained, fewer leaders are available to model.

Those rare models, therefore, are more valuable than we know. We need to seriously evaluate their successes and the ways we can learn from them. Think through the following exercise to help you identify a significant leader who models the principles of Christian marriage we are developing in this book.

1. Choose a husband who exemplifies a style of male headship which centers on developing the spiritual development of his home. Make sure this man is close enough that you can observe and evaluate him.
2. If you draw a blank, find a biography of a spiritual leader from history as a less-than-adequate-but-better-than-nothing starting place.
3. Compare the leader against the principles of family leadership developed so far. Does he view his wife's strengths as complementary? Does he invite her opinions in some sort of executive family management team? Do you see mutual submission in their relationship?
4. What means does this man use to help his family grow spiritually?
5. What are his strengths? What are his weaknesses?

6. What are his wife's strengths and weaknesses?
7. What can you learn from this person? What can you learn from this family's style?

2 You Can't Do It Alone

David

As a minister, I often find myself being asked questions like: "Once and for all, please settle for us, can or cannot a woman hold such-and-such an office in the church?" or "Yes or no, are men and women totally equal?" or "Sure, Paul says in the Bible that the husband is the head of the wife, but what does that precisely mean?"

Answering any of these questions nowadays is a little like tiptoeing through a minefield. That's why we'll pick up our discussion of spiritual leadership in the home right here; it will serve as a broad, foundational base to help us answer questions like those above.

Scripture, I believe, instructs God's people to view the sexes as complementary.

Complimentary with an "i" means to shower praise upon or express admiration for—a good quality, to be sure. But the word complementary with an "e" refers to bringing to completion or perfection, two parts making up a whole. If one part is lacking, there can be no finished product. This complementariness is a basic, scriptural premise when it comes to talking about the mystery of human sexuality.

Scripture instructs God's people to view the sexes as complementary. One sex completes the other. They are parts of a set. Of course, in one sense, a given human can become whole individually as a male or as a female; but in the total scope, the overall view, without woman man is incomplete, and woman also stands in need of man.

Genesis 1:26-27 reads: "Then God said, 'Let us make man in our image, in our likeness, and let them rule over the fish of the sea and the birds of the air, over the livestock, over all the earth, and over all the creatures that move along the ground.' So God created man in his own image, in the image of God he created him; male and female he created them."

The careful wording of this passage implies that as the persons of the Trinity complement one another (yet God is one), even so male and female enhance each other as parts of a whole. Consequently, in Genesis 2 where Eve is made a helper fit for Adam, it does not mean that Adam isn't a helper fit for her as well.

No, the sexes are unique yet mutually dependent parts of humanity. God's original intention that they work together for the benefit of each other as well as for the benefit of the human race is clear. Unfortunately, in practice, this elementary scriptural premise is far too often overlooked.

Now, instead of the tedious (and impossible) task of attempting to illustrate how this principle applies in every detail of human sexuality, I would prefer to suggest generally what this does and does not mean. The generic approach will actually touch on more areas of living, leaving the application to the individual couple. Besides, I'm fearful that the tedium of specifics may quickly land us in territories which only theologians enjoy inhabiting.

In the matter of marriage, God's intention was that the wife would complete her husband—in every way he would benefit by having her as his mate. In her femaleness (whether physical, mental, emotional, spiritual), she would contribute certain elements to the wholeness of their union which he was unable to provide. The reverse would also be true. A husband would complete his wife—in every way she would benefit by having him as her mate. In his maleness (whether physical, mental, emotional, or spiritual) he would contribute certain elements to the wholeness of their union which she could not possibly provide.

The sexes, then, were to be complementary. This is the basic, godly mindset upon which good marriages are to be built. Together we are to be one; our maleness and femaleness blends together for the benefit of the two, for that of any offspring, and for humanity in general.

Perversion of this delicate balance, in one direction or another, is exploitation. Whenever one mate says to the other, "I expect you to give me what I want, but I feel no great obligation to meet your needs," there is sin. The opposite pole is equally wrong. Any leaning which eliminates distinctions and insists on absolute uniformity between the sexes is a perversion of the delicate balance of complementariness.

In marriage, exploitation occurs when either member thinks, *My fulfillment is really more important than yours*. This is a big problem—perhaps a subconscious one—with a large percentage of men. As I look back on the early years of my own marriage, I know I was guilty of such thinking. Professionally, Karen helped me unstintingly in my chosen area of fulfillment, the pastorate; but I didn't respond in turn by aiding her in areas where she wanted to attain fulfillment. To do so never dawned on me!

In the early years of our marriage Karen couldn't

put her finger on what was troubling her in our relationship. There were tears, there was frustration, there was anger. Later she came to identify it quite clearly; her man was exploiting her. In certain ways, her husband was treating her as a non-person!

Now, quite frankly, I never dreamed a wife of mine would ever covet a role beyond that of Mrs. David R. Mains. Ha!

I've learned to make some pretty major adjustments within the last fifteen to twenty years. It's taken time because my bias was more deeply ingrained than I first realized. My characteristic, first response to Karen's plans was, "If you can manage what you have in mind, sweetheart, fine, but I'm really too busy to help you"—a sort of benign, spousal neglect.

It didn't stop Karen. Like the little red hen whose pleas for help went unheeded, she went to work. She began writing, and as her first book became well-received, she began flying here and there on speaking engagements. She took substantial journalistic assignments and served in significant board capacities. As I watched her gifts and abilities develop, I was stretched beyond my early marriage imagination and forced to consider seriously the scriptural mandate of complementariness.

I began to see that this wife of mine was as strong in certain areas as I was in others. She had developed gifts I depended upon. She seemed to be limitless in her ability to grow and she continually surprised me with new undertakings. At the same time she provided a loving environment in our home, was a source of wisdom on parenting, and had become a strong emotional and support base for me. I am challenged by her spiritual hunger, encouraged by her psychological stability, and held accountable by her demands that I not settle for being less than I can be.

I have often wondered if Karen's gifts and contributions to the Kingdom of God might not be more significant, more lasting, and more far-reaching than my own. One of the growing, major concerns of my life has been to help complete Karen so that she will be all that God has created her to be.

Now, I know that the Mains marriage is not the only marriage where this problem of exploitation exists. You wouldn't be thinking that your fulfillment was more important than that of your spouse's, would you?

Choices, Choices

In *American Couples: Money, Work, Sex*, authors Philip Blumstein and Pepper Schwartz speak of a great shift in American culture:

> A common set of questions and challenges confront all "types" of couples today. The changing nature of male and female roles creates problems as couples go about even the most mundane tasks. For example: Who should do what within the household? The question is not simply who cooks, who takes out the trash, and who repairs the leaky faucet. Such task arrangements are really only a small part of the division of chores in a partnership. The larger question is much more profound and less amenable to easy answers. The household provides symbolic occasions for the establishment of territory and authority. Couples are trying to grapple with how men and women, how men and men, how women and women should relate to one another. Where is fairness and justice? What is compromise? What is the "rightful" province of male and female expertise? Whose needs—or perception of needs—will guide the relationship?[1]

1. Philip Blumstein and Pepper Schwartz, *American Couples: Money, Work and Sex*, (New York: William Morrow, 1983).

Of course, one must be careful not to swing the pendulum so far to the other side that absolute uniformity is embraced and legitimate distinctions are eliminated. Even *The Encyclopaedia Britannica* knows better than that.

A supplement to Britannica's *Great Books of the Western World* included an article titled, "The Difference between Men and Women and the Difference It Makes." Ten pages of introductory facts covered not only the unquestioned male/female differences of anatomy, but also such less-known facts as:

- the average male height around the world is about six inches above that of the female.
- the male's muscular potential is far greater.
- the contrasting skeletal structure is easily differentiated.
- her senses are more perceptive than his.
- evidence seems to validate the common belief that sexual hunger is more characteristic of the male than the female.

None of the contributors to this volume disputed these or related statements. Where they disagreed was in explaining *why* such distinctions occur. Were the differences genetically inherent in the sexes, or had they evolved because of cultural expectations? Are men's muscular capabilities greater because this is the way they are by nature, or is it due to the fact that for centuries men have assumed the roles and activities that have allowed them to thus develop?

I don't mean to cavalierly pass through a very hot debate, but most writers take the position that the cause for these sexual distinctions is a combination of inherent ability and cultural conditioning. Obviously, men didn't develop an extra chromosome (named Y) because of cultural expectations. But then, neither have women traditionally been deprived of education because they were inherently less intelligent than men.

Unfortunately, because of the overlap between natural and cultural causes, many puzzles about sexual capabilities are more difficult to analyze than the two examples cited. Yet without obliterating cultural influences, all the experts seem to agree that there are inherent genetic differences between the sexes which influence male/female drives, temperaments, sensitivities, and so on.

Back to my premise. I maintain that males and females were created with many of these contrasts *for the very purpose of complementing one another*. Therefore, any effort to eliminate contrasts perverts God's original intent.

We are not androgynous. Some of us are male, and some of us are female. It is true that there is no distinction before God in terms of our inherent value as human beings—one sex is not valued more by the Creator than the other. Paul lays any such question to rest once and for all when he writes, "You are all sons of God through faith in Christ Jesus . . . There is neither Jew nor Greek, slave nor free, male nor female . . . " (Galatians 3:26, 28).

Still, in stating that men and women are equal before God, the Scriptures also maintain that the male is the head in marriage (Ephesians 5:23). The Bible does not overlook the need for leadership in human relationships. We will look at this key passage more closely a little later, but for now let us see that it instructs men to play their role—for which God has more universally suited them—in the same fashion in which Christ gives leadership to his church.

I don't believe the average Christian wife is going to feel dehumanized if she's married to a husband who sincerely attempts to lead the home in an intelligent, loving, Christlike fashion, asking, "What's best for my spouse? What's best for my children?" That's the arrangement Scripture teaches.

At this point, many "but what ifs" could be raised. I know only too well that sick marriages precipitate these questions, multiplying them everywhere in proliferating numbers. But let me avoid such inquiries because my basic concern is for those relationships that are within a wide range of healthiness but are floundering on the issues of headship.

Are you operating from the awareness that marriage partners are to complement one another? Have you wobbled, in thinking and practice, into the area of exploitation? Does one spouse place greater value on his or her importance? Or are you attempting to achieve absolute uniformity, trying to pretend there aren't really any differences to speak of?

This same kind of examination has broader implications and should be applied to man/woman relationships in both church and society. Does one sex consistently take advantage of the other? That's exploitation. Are all differences eliminated so the terms "male" and "female" relate only to matters of reproduction? That's an unreal insistence on uniformity.

I know it would be impossible to expect all people to agree with this understanding, but I believe I speak with the authority of Scripture that God instructs people to view the sexes as complementary. All of us need to examine our view in relationship to our spouse. Is it based upon this biblical foundation of complementariness?

Successful spiritual leadership in the home flows out of these rich waters. In the next few chapters we will say that Scripture appeals to the privileged to elevate those considered by society to be less privileged; that the whole Ephesians passage on the Christian family comes under the broad heading of mutual submission; that human sexuality cannot be understood without developing a theological concept of mystery; and that the subject of male headship is intertwined with spirituality, with Christ-likeness.

That's a lot of territory to survey, so put on your coonskin hat and get out your canoe. Let's go exploring!

3 The Responsibility of the Privileged

David

Have any of you men ever been accused of being a chauvinist? What man hasn't, these days, in one way or another?

When such abuse is directed my way, I've learned to assume it's probably justified. I'm shifting out of my old stereotypes and considering my flaws. I'm looking carefully at the assumed role of male privilege.

It is a fact that Scripture describes some people as more privileged than others. I didn't say Scripture *appointed* some better than others, just that it recognized some groups had more privileges than others. For example, the Bible considered being a Jew an advantage over being Gentile: "What advantage, then, is there in being a Jew . . . ?" Paul asks in Romans 3. His answer: "Much in every way! First of all, they have been entrusted with the very words of God." Granted, Paul later wrote that the Jewish people were no better off regarding the principle of sin and forgiveness; but at least in terms of the Old Testament narrative, being Jewish was a distinct honor.

Other examples: To be a master was a privilege obviously greater than that of being a slave. And to be a male certainly had advantages over being female. The morning prayer of devout Jewish males during the time of Jesus was, "Blessed art Thou, O Lord God, King of the universe, who has not made me a Gentile. Blessed art Thou, O Lord God, King of the universe, who has not made me a bondsman. Blessed art Thou, O Lord God, King of the universe, who has not made me a woman."

Now, that's chauvinism for you!

It's simply a fact of Scripture that some people were recognized as having advantage over others. This special edge was reflected in Jewish law.

It is also true theologically that such advantages were eliminated by the coming of Christ. That is why Paul writes in Galatians 3, "The law was put in charge to lead us to Christ that we might be justified by faith. Now that faith has come, we are no longer under the supervision of the law. You are all sons of God through faith in Christ Jesus. . . . There is neither Jew nor Greek, slave nor free, male nor female, for you are all one in Christ Jesus."

Let's restate what Paul said: Being Jewish is no longer an advantage over being Gentile; if you're a master who has become a Christian (or a Christ-one), suddenly you're really no better than one of your slaves; and sexually, maleness no longer has precedence over femaleness.

It's true there's a sense of mystery in the way this new freedom relates to God-established patterns such as male headship. We'll talk about that later. But what I would like to do now is to bring old patterns into alignment with the new Christian ideal—and that doesn't always come about instantaneously. Why not? Because privileged people normally won't set aside their given dominance without a fight.

If that's true, then, should those Christians in less

status-privileged positions demand their new rights? More specifically, should Christian slaves throw off their chains? Should believing Gentiles demand respect from the Jewish leaders of the early church? Or would women converts be within their rights to revolt against their domineering husbands?

In Scripture, the answer to these questions is clear. In each case, the underprivileged party is to practice submission: "Wives, submit to your husbands, as is fitting in the Lord"; "Slaves, obey your earthly masters . . . with sincerity of heart and reverence for the Lord"; "Children, obey your parents in everything, for this pleases the Lord" (Colossians 3:18-22).

Why such advice? Two reasons. First, Paul tells Titus it is "so that no one will malign the word of God" (Titus 2:5). In other words, it's not to the advantage of the gospel around the world for people to see the Christian way as something that causes slaves to revolt or wives to rebel.

But second—and this is critically important—this process of change is not to be worked out by inciting underprivileged believers to throw off their bondage, but rather by appealing to the privileged to elevate those of lesser rank for the sake of Christ. Scripture places the burden of fleshing out the law of equal value not on those below, but on those above.

A perfect illustration of this principle is found in the little book of Philemon. As you recall, while in Rome Paul led a man named Onesimus to the Lord. As it turned out, the man was a runaway slave of a Christian owner named Philemon. Onesimus, whose name means "useful," turned out to be exactly that to the imprisoned apostle.

Fine for Paul, but what about the fact that the man was a slave who had deserted his master? Would Paul overlook that? No, he wouldn't. But the great apostle was

The Problem of Backgrounds

Brad and Kathy Anderson were both reared in fundamental Christian homes. Brad is reacting to the legalism of his past and is searching for a broader, less inhibiting means of expressing his personal faith. He feels that his father's black-and-white, have-all-the-answers approach not only stunted his decision-making ability, but also pressured him into choosing a ministerial profession for which he had no real calling and which he has since left for a career in business.

Kathy, however, feels that much in her conservative background was excellent. She is homeschooling their lower grade-level children and is searching for order and a means to spiritually nurture her family in a culture that she views as increasingly chaotic and secularized. Brad agrees that she needs to do her own thing, that she's a "gifted teacher;" but admits the extra responsibility Kathy has assumed puts stressful time constraints on their relationship. Kathy wishes Brad would take a more participatory role in the marriage and the training of the children and is inclined to say, "I want him to be the spiritual head of the house."

convinced that God in his providence had arranged everything; and now, in a simple and powerful letter, Paul would use Onesimus to illustrate for all the ages this principle that I've been developing from Scripture.

Because Paul's letter is short, we'll reproduce it below for ease of study.

> Paul, a prisoner of Christ Jesus, and Timothy our brother, to Philemon our dear friend and fellow worker, to Apphia our sister, to Archippus

our fellow soldier and to the church that meets in your home: Grace to you and peace from God our Father and the Lord Jesus Christ.

I always thank my God as I remember you in my prayers, because I hear about your faith in the Lord Jesus and your love for all the saints. I pray that you may be active in sharing your faith, so that you will have a full understanding of every good thing we have in Christ. Your love has given me great joy and encouragement, because you, brother, have refreshed the hearts of the saints.

Therefore, although in Christ I could be bold and order you to do what you ought to do, yet I appeal to you on the basis of love. I then, as Paul—an old man and now also a prisoner of Christ Jesus—I appeal to you for my son Onesimus, who became my son while I was in chains. Formerly he was useless to you, but now he has become useful both to you and to me.

I am sending him—who is my very heart—back to you. I would have liked to keep him with me so that he could take your place in helping me while I am in chains for the gospel. But I did not want to do anything without your consent, so that any favor you do will be spontaneous and not forced. Perhaps the reason he was separated from you for a little while was that you might have him back for good—no longer as a slave, but better than a slave, as a dear brother. He is very dear to me but even dearer to you, both as a man and as a brother in the Lord.

> So if you consider me a partner, welcome him as you would welcome me. If he has done you any wrong or owes you anything, charge it to me. I, Paul, am writing this with my own hand. I will pay it back—not to mention that you owe me your very self. I do wish, brother, that I may have some benefit from you in the Lord; refresh my heart in Christ. Confident of your obedience, I write to you, knowing that you will do even more than I ask.
>
> And one thing more: Prepare a guest room for me, because I hope to be restored to you in answer to your prayers.
>
> Epaphras, my fellow prisoner in Christ Jesus, sends you greetings. And so do Mark, Aristarchus, Demas and Luke, my fellow workers.
>
> The grace of the Lord Jesus Christ be with your spirit.

The letter speaks for itself. The Bible proclaims that submission is the rule for Christians in subordinate roles; but it doesn't stop with that. There's also a very strong word from God to the believer in the "top spot." In a sentence, Christians in positions of privilege should seek the best for those below them.

Today the key issue is no longer master/slave or Jew/Gentile but male/female. There's no question that men have traditionally held the position of privilege throughout the world. It is also a fact theologically that in Christ all such "advantages" were eliminated. Yet the question remains: "How do we realign old patterns with the new ideal?"

A simple formula can be drawn from Scripture: (1) Women should submit to the given order; (2) men are to bring God's new order into effect.

Don't miss this strong, primary responsibility imposed upon men. In Ephesians, Paul's real appeal is to men to bring Christ's new order into effect. Male followers of Christ are expected to stop exploiting their position. They are to seek the very best for women. They are to encourage women to be all God wants them to be. Christian men are to elevate women to their own status.

Here is where the real problem regarding male/female sexuality lies. Most men have not understood and therefore have not responded to the scriptural instruction. In the community of believers, it's my opinion that women have been far more exemplary in their obedience to Scripture than have men.

Is it possible you are one who needs to examine more closely whether you have concentrated so hard on making sure your sisters in Christ know what God is saying to them that you have missed his clear word to you? Can the phrase "no longer as a slave, but more than a slave" be resaid for today, "no longer a woman, but more than a woman"?

Elevate her! Bestow honor upon her! For her, seek the very best!

If you want to become an effective spiritual leader in your home, it's the best way.

4

Karen

The Quantum Physics of Christian Marriage

The premier passage in all of Scripture dealing with husband/wife relationships is Ephesians 5:21-33. It is one of the most tender portrayals of marital love in all of human literature.

It's also a great treatise on mutual submission. Paul begins his instruction there with the words "Submit to one another out of reverence for Christ." And then he says this:

> Wives, submit to your husbands as to the Lord. For the husband is the head of the wife as Christ is the head of the church, his body, of which he is the Savior. Now as the church submits to Christ, so also wives should submit to their husbands in everything.
>
> Husbands, love your wives, just as Christ loved the church and gave himself up for her to make her holy, cleansing her by the washing with water through the word, and to present her to himself as a radiant church, without stain or

> wrinkle or any other blemish, but holy and blameless. In this same way, husbands ought to love their wives as their own bodies. He who loves his wife loves himself. After all, no one ever hated his own body, but he feeds and cares for it, just as Christ does the church—for we are members of his body. "For this reason a man will leave his father and mother and be united to his wife, and the two will become one flesh." This is a profound mystery—but I am talking about Christ and the church. However, each one of you also must love his wife as he loves himself, and the wife must respect her husband.

The apostle revolutionized the known order and placed upon the shoulders of the male, as spiritual head, the primary responsibility for creating a marriage so harmonious that it mirrors the relationship of Christ to his church. There are three and one-half verses of instruction for the women, and eight and one-half verses for the men. Men are to put away their brutishness and elevate their wives through Christlike self- sacrifice so that an environment of shelter and nourishment and mutuality can be created with her best interest at heart.

Unfortunately, the church still struggles to get Paul's main point. This is not a passage on the subjection of women. If anything, it is a passage which elevates her. Its most elemental message urges males and females, once bound together by the curse of combative sexuality, to discover in loving self-sacrifice a meaning so profound Paul declares it a mystery—something beyond our power of words to explain.

Perhaps a lesson in quantum theory will make these concepts clearer.

When scientists began to observe the microscopic

world, the world of atoms and electrons and protons, they were shocked to discover that the Newtonian physics which applied so well to the macroscopic world of stars and planets and meteors no longer fit.

Newton's laws of motion describe how moving objects should behave, from the orbit of the moon to the spinning of a top. The space program would never have gotten off the ground without Newton's earlier work. Although the calculations for a moon launch are exceedingly complex and by necessity are handled by computer, the mechanics used are basically the ones described in Newton's *Philosophiae Naturalis Principia Mathematica* written in the late 1600s.

This is the world of the macrocosm.

In the world of the microcosm, however, the rules change.

The mind-expanding discovery of quantum mechanics is that Newtonian physics does not apply in the subatomic realm. In a Newtonian equation, we know that "if such-and-such is the case now, and no outside forces interfere, then such-and-such is going to happen next." If we see an airplane flying north at two hundred miles per hour, for example, we know that in one hour it will be two hundred miles farther north (provided it does not change course or speed).

That's not true in the subatomic realm. In the world of quantum mechanics, we cannot precisely know both the position and the momentum of a particle. Let's say you wanted to know something about the momentum of a particle. The only way to gather information about the particle is to shoot beams of light at it; but when you do that, you disturb the particle. The more light you shoot, the more you move the particle out of place, and the less you know about its position. The truth is, we can approximate both position and momentum, but the more we know about one, the less we know about the other. This is Werner Heisenberg's uncertainty principle, a principle which has been verified repeatedly by experiment.

This is not the only aspect of quantum theory which seems to contradict common sense. Such contradictions are at the heart of the new physics. The new physics tells us time and again that the world may not be what we think it is—it may be much, much more.

In a sense, that is what Paul is saying in this Ephesians 5 passage. He is laying out a new and startling order for human relationships, particularly for male and female relationships, and most specifically for husbands and wives. Paul is saying, "Because of Christ, and because of his life within us, things are no longer what they once seemed. The world of marriage is not what we think it is. In fact, it is much, much more."

The very writing of this passage is one of common-sense contradictions, of complementary parallels that seemingly don't touch. Paul strikes a delicate and intricate balance: "Wives, submit . . . Husbands, love . . . each one of you also must love his wife as he loves himself, and the wife must respect her husband." All of these duties are bound up in Christ.

Paul's point is that being chief is not the point. We cannot look at the new spiritual order with our old, pagan concepts regarding human relationships. Being boss over, being the superior, being the household authority, being a human demi- god—none have anything to do with this passage. Christian marriage is not like the Newtonian order, where truth is either/or, where if such-and-such is such-and-such, it cannot be so-and-so; or where if man is head, then woman must be servant.

Paul is not so much concerned with a human hierarchy as he is with the experience and demonstration of a new spiritual order. In this realm, where man must lose his life in order to gain it (another true, commonsense contradiction), nothing will ever be the same again.

Let me give another example. The particle theory of light says light is made up of tiny packages of energy called photons which travel along paths of least resistance, usually in straight lines like bullets. The theory has been substantiated experimentally and was a tremendous achievement in the world of higher physics. The only problem is that some one hundred years before the particle theory was developed, an Englishman named Thomas Young had shown that light is made up of waves which travel in wavelength frequencies. Experiments also confirm his theory.

Today's higher physics accepts both models and conceives of light as a wave-particle duality. It is a commonsense contradiction, but seems true nonetheless. Light is both wave and particle. The observer can examine its wave nature or its particle nature—but not both at once. And although only one side can be adequately observed at one time, the observer must keep in mind the tension between wave and particle in order to really understand the nature of light.

So it is with the quantum physics of Christian marriage. The world is not what it seems to be. In reality it is much, much more.

The passage in Ephesians 5 is not to be looked at through the eyes of our old, unredeemed understanding. The coming of Christ and his life and death have ushered in a new order. And it is an order we must keep in proper tension.

Two distinct realities must be acknowledged if the physics of marriage is to be understood. One is the function of the husband—a sacrificial kind of loving, spiritual leadership. The other is the function of the wife—a healing kind of strength that stems from the willing gift of respect.

Both are wrapped together in an atom called "submit to one another."

Many partners in marriage soon discover an inordinate need to be in control. They discover that mutual submission is very hard. At the same time, many others are beginning to suspect that it is this very practice that holds a key to human freedom. Still others have learned that they have submitted too much and in the wrong ways; they see that what they once termed submission was in reality appeasement or subservience, and they are beginning to suspect that the two are not the same.

Christ, our model of submission, is the One who drove the money changers out of the temple, who denounced the Pharisees for their hypocrisy, who defied the legalists and healed on the Sabbath, and who refused to lay down his life before the proper time set by his Father. He was always shattering the old, impoverished orders—a divine-human challenging old preconceptions with commonsense contradictions.

It's perfectly appropriate when looking at this Ephesians passage to ask, "What kind of husband would Christ be? What kind of wife?" In fact, it's only when we begin to explore the answer to this question that old and inadequate ways of looking at the world begin to die and that we find the courage to discard our faulty masculine and feminine prejudices. Only then can Christ shine through the print on the Ephesian pages of our Scripture. Only then can we begin to understand the Pauline "new physics of marriage."

5
Karen

Submission Is like Shoveling Snow off the Roof

If the new order for Christian marriage is something like the principles of higher physics, then mutual submission is a lot like shoveling snow off the roof.

In the winter of 1979, the Chicago area received what was euphemistically called a "dump" by local weather forecasters. Our neighborhood endured such a record snowfall that our children were literally jumping off the roof into huge nearby drifts of snow.

So much snow piled up on the housetop that ice jams formed at the roofline and soon melted upon contact with the warm attic air. Rivulets of cold water leaked first from the bedroom dormers, then through the struts, next in yellow streaks down the newly-painted basement walls, and finally followed a path of least resistance to drip from the middle of the living room and dining room ceilings. At one point, some twenty pans, bowls, and vases caught the persistent deluge.

The Mains family attacked the problem with shovels in hand and, like many of our neighbors (despite the warnings of local orthopedic surgeons), took to the roof!

Up went the ladders. Up scrambled David and the teen-agers. Up scrambled my daughter and myself followed by the two little boys. We were bundled in winter coats and scarves, double pairs of thermal stockings, and we began our work at the peak line.

"Watch out!" I cried. "Don't fall off the roof!"

David tied ropes around the waists of those who were working close to the edges, then attached the other end in a tight circle around the chimney. The work continued all morning, and despite the leaking house, it is one of my fonder family memories. There was such a happy camaraderie in that gargantuan work project (the snow was three feet deep).

"Don't get overtired, now," we would say to one another. "Better take a break." "Is anyone cold? Go get warmed up."

Up and down the ladder we climbed. Someone made hot chocolate and the work became an outdoor picnic. "Hey, Mom! Look at me!" And the first brave soul jumped off the roof into a nearby drift, only to be followed in quick succession by the others.

"Better go inside," David would say to me as he shoveled snow precariously near the edge. (It was one thing to take a well-planned jump into a nearby drift; it was another to lose one's balance and fall.) "I don't want you overexerting yourself."

And I, thinking of the risk of heart attacks in snow-shoveling, underexercised middle-aged men would say, "No, I'm good for another half hour. How are you doing?"

Finally, after a morning of work and laughter, after aching muscles and blistered hands and frozen feet, the roof was clean. The snow had been shoveled, the ice pack had been pounded clear. We all convened in the kitchen for bowls of hot chili, and with the most sublime satisfaction, I noticed that the dripping in the house was becoming slower and slower, and—oh joy!—it finally stopped.

The drywall would not crumble more, the ceilings would not fall. We could empty the pots and pans and put them all away.

Shoveling the roof has become one of those classic family memories: "Remember the year we shoveled the roof? Remember how it snowed so much we actually jumped off the roof into drifts?"

I seem to be the only one who remembers the leaking walls and the twenty pots and pans.

The year we shoveled the roof taught us that when a huge task is at hand, a whole family has to pull together to get the work done. The Ephesians 5 passage on marriage reminds me of this episode in our family life. My Revised Standard Version Bible headlines Ephesians 5:21-6:9 as "The Christian household," and so it is—a description of relationships between husbands and wives, children and parents, slaves and masters. The instructions that guarantee harmonious family life begin with this one command, "Submit to one another out of reverence for Christ." The rest of the chapter unfolds a picture of mutual submission.

Why do we have such a difficult time understanding what mutual submission looks like? Maybe it's because many families never have had to shovel snow off the roof.

That is mutual submission. It's having a task so huge, so enormous, that the effort of the entire family is required. The task of each Christian couple is to create a home that has a spiritual environment, one that is Christ-centered, that models what God intended for society to be like (be it ever so small a microcosm), a place on earth that will generate health, warmth, security, and stability for all who dwell therein.

Mutual submission is caring that others don't fall off the roof. It's pulling your fair share of the work. It's being concerned about one another's strained muscles and blistered fingers and frostbitten toes. It's climbing down

Whose Style Is Right?

Sheree and Daniel Brubaker have been married for seven years. Daniel never knew his natural father, who abandoned the family early in the marriage. Daniel's mother has been divorced several times and he was reared haphazardly, with the confusing example of several step-fathers. Daniel became a Christian in college, met Sheree and was attracted to the order, care and stability of her church-going family.

Although Sheree's family past was stable and loving, Sheree nevertheless is now exploring new territory different from the traditional ground staked out by her mother. A college graduate with a career in physical therapy, Sheree plans to re-enter her field after their two small children are in school. Her mind is active and her interests wide-ranging; this is in contrast to her mother who has been content with a smaller circuit of hearth and church.

Daniel has difficulty even imagining the role a Christian husband and father plays in the home, and Sheree asks, "Can't there be two leaders in a home? All my old tapes, the sermons, the Bible teaching say, 'No!' But is that really so? Why can't two people pull together?"

the ladder and fixing hot chocolate simply because you're the one who's too cold for roof duty and who can get warm in the kitchen and do a useful task at the same time. It's making the job fun by inventing a jumping-off-the-roof game. It's the common satisfaction of a roof cleared of snow and ice followed by the reassuring knowledge that the windows and ceilings and walls are no longer dripping water. It's creating a safe environment against the hazards of outside atmospheric hostility.

Mutual submission is having a task so gigantic that everyone must pull together using whatever muscle, strength, and ingenuity is available in order to get the task done.

One of the interests of the Mains family is good theater. Our children loved the play *The Skin of Our Teeth* by Thornton Wilder. Wilder portrays the institution of the family throughout history from the ice age to modern times—all in one evening through an absurdly serious dramatization. Wilder wrote the play in 1939 while Shanghai was being occupied by the Japanese, when Austria fell to Hitler's forces, and while the Spanish Republicans were about to be overwhelmed by Franco's fascists. Wilder's biographer, Gilbert Harrison, says the play "was an attempt to answer the universal question: When a human being is made to bear more than a human being can bear, what then?"

Wilder wanted to declare explicitly and resoundingly that whatever the cataclysms—ice age, flood, wars—mankind would go on: "Let us be willing to pass through fear, doubt and abandon in order to be stronger in courage, faith and love." Gilbert Harrison again: "In *The Skin of Our Teeth*, he wanted to chart mankind's wrong turnings, dead ends, pain, treachery, brutality, absurdities, while simultaneously underlining the fact of human endurance."[1]

Wilder intended that his fictitious clan, the Antrobus family, should represent civilization at large; but isn't it interesting that it is the family itself which has preserved society in the face of cataclysm, disaster, and tumult beyond mankind's control?

Mutual submission works at creating a *home*, the kind of place each person holds in his or her heart as an ideal of what shelter, security, and nurture should be. The very word creates an emotional longing in us—a place to go when the spirit of adventure has waned, a place to return to when the world presses and headlines blare and marketplace competition tears us to pieces.

This is the monumental task for each Christian couple which will require mutual labor, mutual dreaming, mutual submission. Did you know Paul sprinkles clues in his letter as to how to accomplish this?

> Children, obey your parents *in the Lord* . . .
>
> Fathers . . . bring [your children] up in the training and instruction *of the Lord* . . .
>
> Slaves, obey . . . with respect and fear, and with sincerity of heart, *just as you would obey Christ . . . like slaves of Christ, doing the will of God* from your heart. Serve wholeheartedly, *as if you were serving the Lord*, not men . . .
>
> Masters . . . you know that *he who is both their Master and yours is in heaven*, and there is no favoritism with him.

One Saturday morning in February I awoke with the heavy cloud of my feeble humanity hanging over my head. Depression sat on my bedcovers and wagged its doleful finger at me. I had done everything wrong. The catalogue of my inadequacies was more than I could bear. I had missed deadlines. I felt I was a lousy writer. Despite my best attempts to be accurate, I had misquoted some resource material and had brought down upon my head the wrath of certain radio listeners. David was having to unscramble my checkbook again—wouldn't I ever grow up?—and on and on.

I lay in bed, seriously considering the possibility of canceling that February day, of putting my head under the covers and sleeping through it. But I thought, "No, this is Saturday. This is the day on which we have been trying to teach the children how to get ready to welcome

Christ's presence into our hearts and homes so that we can welcome him into church on Sunday. I can wallow in my fragile, failing humanity, or I can 'Christify' this day." I followed my own advice, limped out of bed, and before too long my attitude was radically transformed (to the family's great relief).

In his book, *The Table of Inwardness*, author Calvin Miller talks about "Christifying" each moment. And though it sounds mystical, it's really quite a pragmatic process. It is as simple as lying in bed with ruinous emotions and choosing instead to make Christ the focus of a gray, overbearing February day.

This is what Paul is saying in this passage: Christify your household, let everything you do be "of Christ, in Christ, as Christ, to Christ." Mutual submission in a unit such as the family begins with this understanding. We must all attempt to Christify our relationships with each other.

So how do we get the whole crew, our Christian families, to shovel snow off the roof so that the leaking in the household will stop? First, we must realize we have a gargantuan undertaking at hand—the creation of a Christian home. Second, we must choose to Christify each moment that we live together. We must choose to Christify our family relationships, and we must teach each other by example to do the same.

That is the beginning of a process that results in the finished product of mutual submission. It's like saying, "The house is leaking. We've got to shovel the snow off the roof. We must work together to accomplish the task. And we can have fun doing it."

In fact, every day in most families, there's a snow-shoveling job of some kind. The task can be handled in the worst of ways, or it can be handled in the best of ways by Christifying our interaction with each other.

Mutual submission—working together—is the best of ways Paul knew. He also knew that working together begins by seeking to Christify our family relationships.

To the roofs!

NOTES

1. Gilbert Harrison, *The Enthusiast: A Life of Thornton Wilder* (New Haven: Ticknor & Fields, 1983), pp. 195-196.

Couples' Discussion Questions

When the next roof-shoveling task comes your way, talk over these questions with each other.

1. How can we Christify this situation?
2. How can we Christify the language we will use with each other as we communicate about this dreary moment?
3. How can we Christify our attitude toward each other?

6 A Profound Mystery

David

"Daddy," my children asked when they were little, "if Jesus was alive before he came to earth, when was he really born?"

Now, the correct answer is easy to give; but for a young daughter or son to understand, that is another matter. How can someone always have been alive, and still have to be born? That's confusing.

Sifting through the problem of time and eternity, however, is just the beginning. As my children grew, they had to deal with issues such as God existing as one but also as three; or the issue of Christ being 100 percent human while also being 100 percent divine. And there are others: Did God choose me, or did I choose him? If God already knows what's going to happen, then why should I have to pray? Before we know it, we're into problems too big even for adults to comprehend.

It's very important to understand that this is not a stage one eventually outgrows. Just the opposite is true. The sooner a person comes to realize that these puzzles are part of our faith, the more comfortable he or she is going to be.

But I fear this is difficult for the western mind to accept. We tend to demand that every issue be resolved tightly with no loose ends, and we suppose that once the appropriate facts are obtained all contradictions will vanish. The problem is that such a position trumpets man's intellect as supreme and insists that God must fit into the categories humans can understand.

In Scripture, however, the word "mystery" appears frequently. It implies that our inability to comprehend every element of truth in no way invalidates that truth's apparently contradictory elements. The fact is, the great principles about God and his creation are always too wonderful to dissect the way we might a worm or a frog. It's a mystery that God is one but three; it's a mystery that his choice is what matters in salvation, but so does ours; and so on. . . .

Interestingly enough, Paul comes to the end of his crucial passage on male/female relationships in Ephesians 5:32 and says, "This is a profound mystery." "This"—meaning husband/wife relationships—"is a profound mystery." The Amplified Bible renders it, "This mystery is very great."

Unfortunately, this passage is also the one used again and again by supposed students of the Bible to fit male/female into a package that's completely comprehensible and sealed neatly for all time. Certain folks have a compelling need to eliminate the mystery. But it won't work; the phrase stands there like a mountain of granite: "This is a profound mystery."

The truth is, no matter how much you study this topic, there's still a certain enigma about how the sexes are related. They're the same but they're not the same. They're equal but they're also not equal. They're one and united, and then again they're separate and distinct.

Which Oars Do You Pull?

Andrea and Richard Miller both come from non-church backgrounds. After becoming Christians they met and married and have no children. Andrea is a businesswoman with her own insurance firm. "I put Richard through grad school so he could teach business at the grad level. The pressure on me for the responsibility of making our living was really rough. I vowed that I didn't want to foist that sole role upon my husband once he was through school, that I would always try to earn some part of our family income."

Both Millers were reared in families with severe disruptive elements: alcoholism, emotional abandonment, abusive authoritarianism. "Trust is an issue with me," admits Andrea. "Because the authority of my childhood was so disordering—the bull-in-a-china-shop variety—it is now difficult to trust anyone. I react negatively to the very word 'authority.'" Richard elaborates, laughing a little at himself: "We think a marriage should be two people pulling on the oars together; the only problem is that we don't know which oars!"

Differences can be shown by beginning with the obvious— men's and women's bodies are not the same. Likeness can be demonstrated in their equal value before God. But it would be impossible to get consensus on the question, "Where should the lines be drawn that begin separating how they are alike from how they are different?"

I believe this realm of male/female relationships is another of those areas which forces us to admit our human limitations and to say, "To God alone belongs such ultimate wisdom." It is a profound mystery.

"But how can I live with mystery?" someone is bound to ask.

I always give the same answer. First, we live with mystery by accepting it for what it is; and second, by knowing what to do with it.

First, let us learn to accept mystery. When I use the term, I'm not implying that all life is a hopeless jumble of impossible-to-correlate facts. No, I'm only affirming that life does contain mysteries beyond our ability to plumb. There are questions we cannot comprehend exhaustively, and human sexuality is one. Now, if we can accept this, we can go on.

How, then, can we know what to do when we come across these areas of seeming contradiction? As simple as it sounds, we merely stress the side of truth that common sense tells us is needed in the given environment.

In nineteenth-century America, for example, God's sovereignty had been emphasized so strongly that a doctrinal misinterpretation had developed. The scriptural emphasis on man's responsibility was sorely neglected. Charles Finney, the great revivalist, began preaching that each person was responsible for his actions. His teaching helped precipitate a wide, sweeping revival which culminated in enormous social reform.

Finney's emphasis helped give birth to the abolitionist movements of William Lloyd Garrison and Thomas Weld, both young protégés. Recent sociological studies focusing upon the area of upper New York state indicate that a decade of intense revivalism, from 1825-1837, produced every major reform movement of the nineteenth century. The temperance movement, the missionary and Bible societies which carried the gospel across the country and all the way to China, a reform of sabbath observance, education reform movements devoted to propagating literacy and establishing free schools, the feminist movement—all these issued from calls like Finney's to personal responsibility.

Profound societal shifts took place largely because Finney redressed the imbalance in one theological position; he taught that man is responsible for his own actions. Did Finney, by doing so, cease to believe that God chooses whom he wills? No. Did Finney know how the two fit together? If he did, he didn't preach about it. He simply began to balance what had become an unhealthy extreme.

What does this mean in relation to human sexuality, the topic at hand? Simply this: Knowing what to do when confronted with biblical mysteries helps unravel the problem of sexual roles.

In marriage, for example, Scripture teaches that the male partner is the head. Whatever else that means—and the word in the original language carries a range of meaning—"head" certainly includes the idea of the husband being "over" his wife. At the same time, however, the Bible says that in Christ there is no longer a difference between male and female (Galatians 3:28). Scripture seems to be teaching that there is a difference and that there is not a difference. That's what I call (and what Paul teaches is) a profound mystery.

How do you deal with mystery? You emphasize whichever side of the truth is most lacking in the situation.

How can you tell which side needs emphasizing? Being the pragmatic theologian that I am, I say, "Use common sense."

Maybe you could use an example. Let's say that here's a marriage between Christians in which chaos reigns and where each partner is tearing at the other. What would I stress in that situation? I would stress headship, and I would do so not because it is the ultimate answer, but because some kind of form or structure or law is required to restore order. If both parties will agree to submit to what this part of Scripture says, recognizing the man as the head of the house will work wonders. That is the element of God's truth which those involved in a disharmonious marriage need to hear.

But what happens when the rocky relationship has stabilized and some harmony and godliness are established? Then it's time to emphasize the other part of God's truth and shift toward greater equality. At that point it's time to apply the scriptural mandate to mutually build up one another and to give full heed to the Bible's enormous consideration for women. You don't give the heave-ho to male headship—that's a biblical constant—but you do seek for ways to make the marriage a true partnership of equals.

My own marriage has become a most egalitarian relationship. Karen and I are co-regents of equal but differing strengths, ruling together.

Do I then cease to be head of my house? Hardly. It's just that the emphasis on the side of truth that establishes order is no longer necessary. Karen and I have learned that lesson and are fleshing out a broader and richer understanding of the other side of the mystery.

The situation dictates which aspect of the biblical mystery is most appropriate to stress—freedom or law, equality or hierarchy, functioning as a leadership team or more under the direction of the husband. Do not misunderstand; this is *not* situational ethics, where truth is jettisoned for the sake of circumstances. Rather, this is an appropriation of whichever element of Scripture most needs to be emphasized at the time, all the while holding the whole truth in tension.

Let me put it this way. No pastor can tell his people what exact percent of their time should be spent working as contrasted to the percent of time they should pray. Both work and prayer are important. The ultimate, appropriate percentages of work and prayer remain a mystery. If the pastor's parishioners do nothing but pray, he must preach on the need for coupling action with contemplation. If they're hyperactive but know nothing of supernatural empowering, he must emphasize the necessity of getting on their knees.

In marriages where the battle of the sexes is still hot, I would say an emphasis on headship is the appropriate "word from the Lord." But where that message has been proclaimed and stressed and heard, it's time to preach about husbands encouraging their wives, about church men inviting women to be all that God wants them to be.

Certainly this makes more sense than emphasizing just one side of the mystery again and again and again and remaining wholly silent about the other side. That is surely an error in judgment, if not also in doctrine.

"This mystery is great," to be sure. But it can also provide rich soil for growing a mature, healthy, productive union in Christ. Are you willing to tackle the mystery? Which side do you need to emphasize? For the sake of your marriage and for the sake of God's Kingdom, spend some time mulling it over and discussing it with your spouse.

And then get to work!

7

Karen

Stretching between the Flagpoles

Here I stand in the middle of the mystery of human sexuality.

One hand stretches to grasp a flagpole secured firmly in the earth beside me. The banner that flaps from its tip bears the design of male headship with its nuances of order and authority.

My other hand struggles to grasp the opposite pole, anchored as firmly as the first. Halyard clanging, this staff flies the standard of equality of the sexes, the utter co-relationship of man and woman through the miracle of the continuing incarnation of the God-man, Christ.

I stand here, woman that I am, frequently uncomfortable, mentally spread-eagled, pinioned between two basic, scriptural tenets that seem opposite each other, refusing to bow together despite my efforts. The changing winds of theological exposition blow. Headship I can only reach with my fingertips; equality is almost beyond my grasp.

My shoulders ache.

I am painfully aware that my between-pole-standing will please few. I am neither feminist nor anti-feminist, and I look ridiculous in my struggle to hold on to both flagpoles. Although in some ways I am laughable, that is often the nature of truth—especially spiritual truth. In spite of the best of my rational efforts, I am often left touching paradox when what I most wish for is firm conclusion.

Truth often has this elusive quality. It refuses satisfaction like that which comes from a completed jigsaw puzzle on the dining room table. Somehow, the pieces don't all fit, and some seem obviously missing.

Take the incarnation. How can Christ be both God and man? Surely he is either one or the other. How about a ratio of 60 percent to 40 percent? Or of 80 percent to 20 percent?

Or how can we be foreordained and yet be individually responsible? How can Scripture be both human and divine? How can communion be both natural and supernatural—is it symbol or miracle?

Because we live in the twentieth century, with the arguments of the early church fathers behind us, we understand the folly of such mental gymnastics. What we don't understand is that we are already living comfortably with mystery, that we *are* standing between poles, squarely in the middle between opposites—the supernatural and the human.

Firm flagpoles such as these stand all over biblical terrain, the rallying points for doctrinal disputations.

Do not think that I am against rational struggle; on the contrary, I enjoy healthy, theological inquiry. I am becoming aware, however, that if intellectual investigation does not allow for the paradoxical, for the mysterious, for the incomprehensible, it leads to arrogance, a dominant sin in the church. It lurks in my own heart.

So I am concerned that much of the discussion concerning women is floundering in hazy doctrine when it should be majoring in pragmatics. There has never been a more dramatic time to minister to women because of thinking stimulated by the pros and cons of the feminist movement.

That the church is still discussing the "changing" role of women shows how woefully unaware we are of what has already happened. For all practical purposes, the role of women has already changed, and ministry is obliged to deal with what now exists. The working woman, for example, represents one dynamic aspect of this change.

Times Have Changed

The adult life expectancy of women has more than doubled during the twentieth century. The life expectancy of the female infant born in 1900 in the United States was forty-eight; today it is close to eighty. The adult years of women were thereby doubled from twenty-eight to sixty years. American mothers averaged 7.5 children when the first census was taken in 1790; by 1965 this average had dropped to 2.3, and by 1986 it was up to 2.67. Bearing children early in their marriage, this often meant that by age twenty-six a mother's childbearing years were ended. By age forty—with life expectancy but half completed and remaining mature years but one-third completed—basic maternal tasks were over. The modern woman could no longer be categorized as a lifetime mother.

Despite the difficulties of this complicated discussion on male/female roles, David and I prefer not to fall out on one side or the other of the issue. We prefer to maintain the muscle-stretching act that comes from trying to grasp the halyard of both these doctrinal poles. Holding firmly to both headship and mutual value does exactly what I have described: As a couple we are stretched, challenged, in tension, evolving, non-static, forced into dynamic growth.

Euripides said, "Woman is woman's natural ally." While that may often have been true down the centuries, the church can no longer afford to perpetuate such an attitude, intentionally or otherwise. Feminist issues are too crucial for pet positions that do not reflect Christ.

Jesus allowed a prostitute to embrace him publicly. He refused to chide a woman with a "female disease" when she clutched at his clothes. He showed tender compassion for a bereaved widow. He allowed all those middle-aged, neurotic, menopausal types to be a part of his inner band of disciples and to minister to his needs.

The amazing truth is that Christ, who is our example, loved woman. There is no room for hidden misogyny in his followers. The Christian man cannot hate mother or wife or daughter or sister. The feminist cannot hate the woman who does not adopt her own thinking. The proponents of male headship cannot disdain those who adamantly espouse equality. Neither dare we hate the *anima*, the feminine self of our own being, whether we are man or woman. Hatred for women is antithetical to Christ. It is evil perpetrated toward a human half of the creation our Lord holds dear.

All discussions and all final opinions about male/female roles, conservative or liberal, must be rooted firmly and primarily in the example of Christ as revealed in the Gospels. Until our doctrine is similarly grounded in that kind of love, we will limit our understanding of how men and women are to function in marriage with each other . . . no matter which pole of truth we rally around.

I personally need that kind of Christlike love, not only from David, but from the Christian men in my church and from those in the broader community of faith. I need them to teach me more of what Christ's love is like as they extend it to me. And I want to return that divine favor. I want to be part of that new society of love and righteous purity modeled in the Gospels and delineated in the Epistles.

As a teenager some thirty-odd years ago, I wore no make-up and carried my red Bible on top of my school books. I quizzed with a Youth for Christ memorization team, helped run a Pioneer Girls' club in my church, gave off-handed nods to academics, involved myself in student council, and read whenever I could steal precious moments for myself. I had no inkling of the incredible revolution in thought regarding my role as a woman that was to challenge my generation in the ensuing decades.

My life today traces a circuit of recording studio, production meetings, laundry room, editorial conferences, extended family celebrations with new in-laws and my college children's friends, writing desk, prayer closet, church board and extensive travel responsibilities. I would have seen myself doing few of these activities when I was a high schooler in the fifties.

Since then I have learned to say no; to outline a radio broadcast while jogging; regretfully to limit my circle of friends; to think at odd moments; to minister to a few through counseling; to maintain prayer notebooks; to answer my correspondence promptly; to work on keeping my marriage lively; to listen completely when the children talk to me; to involve myself in choice, heartfelt causes; to strike a well-needed balance between contemplation and activism. I agree with that friend who sighed, "The opportunities for women are expanding so quickly, it's enough to destroy you."

In the middle of all this, I'm undone when a male says to me, "Hey, friend, are you sure *you're* doing OK? Is there anything I can do for you? Is there any way I can remember you in prayer?" My past has prepared me for sermons from 1 Timothy 2:11-15 (on submissiveness, silence, and pushy women). I am not prepared for those rare males who know how to live out the Christlike love of 1 Timothy 5:1-3, a brotherly love for women in the body with all purity. What an incredible ministry they have to the modern woman, whether in the context of marriage or in broader church life!

Often I would like to throw the whole discussion of human sexuality out the window, and about half the time I do, forgetting myself and that I am female. The other half of the time it is all I think about. It intrigues me, fascinates me, frustrates me, eludes my understanding. It is the source of all my feelings about myself. But the more my need to hold it firmly, the more it mocks me.

So I return to mystery, and I stand uncomfortably in the tension of the paradox of "male and female he created them." I stretch my arms to the two poles, shaking my head and exclaiming with the apostle Paul, who expressed wonder at the male/female roles in marriage: "This mystery is a profound one. . . ."

Can any of us ultimately conclude anything else?

8 In Christ, To Christ, For Christ

David

A close look at Ephesians 5:21-33 reveals some interesting phrases. If the phrases were red yarn, they would wind brightly in and out of the pages of our Bibles: "Out of reverence for Christ," "as to the Lord," "as Christ is the head of the church," "as the church submits to Christ," "as Christ loved the church and gave himself up for her," "as Christ does the church," "I am talking about Christ and the church."

One can't study this passage seriously without seeing the bright skein that binds the marriage together. It is Christ, in Christ, as to Christ, through his example, for Christ.

Living for Christ is good preparation for marriage, and living out a good marriage is an excellent discipline that expands our growth in Christ.

Let me emphatically say in this sexually loose age that Christians have no need to apologize about their moral and ethical spiritual roots. An active, obedient faith stands us all in very good stead when it comes to creating a successful married life. In fact, some valuable lessons can be learned in the walk of faith that apply directly to the wedded state.

For example, maturing Christians have become accustomed to making an unreserved commitment to God. They know it's folly to say, "I give myself totally to you, God, except. . . ." They know they're not perfect, but they've learned to pray with the hymn writer, "Lord, take my life, and make it wholly thine." This practice of unconditional surrender to God can't help but have healthy implications in marriage.

For the most part, unreserved commitment to anything but one's self is a tough lesson for the average man or woman on the street. Contemporary human loyalties tend to be conditional. Pledges are made with mental reservations. Trial marriages are discussed: "Let's hope for the best and see how things go." Lifetime vows are more than many are prepared to keep.

Living for Christ before marriage and within the framework of marriage is good preparation on the human level because it teaches us the lesson of unreserved commitment to something other than ourselves.

Maturing Christians also know that spiritual growth comes gradually. Those who have walked miles with Jesus harbor no illusions of instant spiritual maturity. They look back and see the long road that leads them toward becoming the people God wants them to be. It would be easy to become discouraged by this hindsight view, except that they see how far they've already come.

I'm glad I'm not the person I was five years ago, and I'm delighted this process of growth will continue. The maturing Christian realizes he or she is in the long, sometimes arduous, but wholly satisfying process of growth.

That isn't what our world likes to hear. It demands more and more instant gratification: "I want this-and-that, and I intend to have it right now!" We've developed instant coffee, microwave dinners, condensed books and one-minute car washes, but nobody's been able to package overnight marriage miracles. That fantasy exists only on the silver screen: Boy meets girl, they feel the tingle of love, they jump in bed, and live happily ever after—circumventing courtship, weddings and lifetime marriage altogether. Unfortunately, not only are the viewers of this charade unable to duplicate its neat celluloid tricks, but the actors and actresses who play the parts find themselves powerless to make the story line work out in their off-screen lives.

Those who follow Christ have a much better chance at accomplishing the Bible's odd mathematics of marriage, of making two become one. Why? Because such people bring an expectation of gradual growth to their marriage. They expect time to act as their friend as they live together. Such a mindset not only carries them past unexpected setbacks, but also gives them an assurance that added years of maturing can only better their current condition.

Maturing Christians also know the importance of communication in a spiritual lifestyle. Two-way sharing with God is vital if the human/divine relationship is to remain alive. Growing believers respond to the promptings of the indwelling Holy Spirit. They don't let prayerless days pile up. They train themselves to hear God's voice as they meditate on the Scriptures, for they know these disciplines are the very lifeblood of their spiritual existence.

What incredible implications this discipline has for the marital relationship! Any marital counselor will report that a breakdown in communication is the most common problem of marriages in trouble.

I believe the person who has learned the importance of communication in one major area of life (the spiritual)

A Barren Spiritual Landscape

Allan Bloom, in his watershed book *The Closing of the American Mind*, charges modern academia with moral failure and intellectual impoverishment. Here is part of his analysis:

The gods never walked very tall in our political life or in our schools. The Lord's Prayer we mumbled in grade school when I was a child affected us less than the Pledge of Allegiance we also recited. It was the home— and the houses of worship related to it—where religion lived. The holy days and the common language and set of references that permeated most households constituted a large part of the family bond and gave it a substantial content. Moses and the Tables of the Law, Jesus and his preaching of brotherly love, had an imaginative existence. Passages from the Psalms and the Gospels echoed in children's heads. Attending church or synagogue, praying at the table, were a way of life, inseparable from the moral education that was supposed to be the family's special responsibility in this democracy. Actually, the moral teaching was the religious teaching. There was no abstract doctrine. The things one was supposed to do, the sense that the world supported them and punished disobedience, were all incarnated in the biblical stories. The loss of the gripping inner life vouchsafed those who were nurtured by the Bible must be primarily attributed not to our schools or political life, but to the family, which, with all its rights to privacy, has proved unable to maintain any content of its own. The dreariness of the family's spiritual landscape passes belief. It is as monochrome and unrelated to those who pass through it as are the barren steppes frequented by nomads who take their mere subsistence and move on.[1]

1. Allan Bloom, *The Closing of the American Mind*, (New York: Simon and Schuster, 1987), pp. 56-57.

can easily transfer it to a second area (the marital). Working on one's spiritual life will enhance one's marriage.

Seasoned Christians also have learned the secret of submission in conflicts. They know that when their desires are contrary to God's, insisting on their own way does not bring happiness. Paradoxically, it is in surrendering to God that personal fulfillment comes. Christians who have learned to submit know the power of its surprising truth.

In the world apart from Christ, whether it be nations or spouses, submitting to someone else seems unbearable, distasteful. Rivals follow ancient tribal codes of warfare and believe that confrontations are for winning. But when one bloodied opponent finally stands astride a beaten, battered foe, the victory usually costs more than it's worth. Who really won? Was the devastation worth the territory? Does the benefit to survivors offset the cost in loss of life?

Conflicts are inevitable in human relationships. But, oh how they shrink in size and number when men and women learn to say (and mean) the magic words, "This time I'll submit to your wishes; no, I really want to!" Such sentiments don't threaten those who have learned that, more often than not, the words result in greater happiness, greater harmony, greater unanimity.

Christians are not the same as people of the world. This has been the scriptural position since the beginning of the New Testament church. Christian marriages are not like non-religious marriages. Paul writes in 1 Thessalonians 4:4, 5: "Each of you should learn to control his own body in a way that is holy and honorable, not in passionate lust like the heathen, who do not know God." Our marital relationships are holy, and they are holy because our Christian commitments make them so.

A short while back I was to meet a friend in an unfamiliar town. I thought I had followed his directions properly, but after some time I didn't seem to be where I thought I should be. I pulled into a gas station and asked the attendant for help. "Oh, you're right on track," he said, "only one more block to go." That reassured me and made me feel good.

In a world that loudly shouts the opposite, Christian couples need to know that by following a Christian lifestyle and by developing their spiritual selves and by obeying Christ in difficult areas, they will reap untold benefits in their married lives.

I have said that Paul weaves Christ in and out of the Ephesians passage on marriage, but couples today often have trouble knowing what that means to their marriage. They want to know what it would look like. They need to see models.

Joan Brown in her book *Wings of Joy* displays one of these models from American history.

> The charming colonial house on King street in Northampton, Massachusetts, was more than a house. It was a warm, loving, but often tempestuous home. To many a traveler, the sight of the latchstring hanging outside the front door meant a welcome and endearing hospitality. One of America's greatest preachers and theologians, the Reverend Jonathan Edwards, brought life and love to the bricks and mortar which were used in the construction.
>
> Jonathan Edwards was a loving, impassioned, unpredictable and trying man, often given to depression. Sarah loved him in a very wonderful way. She knew his shortcomings, but realized the genius that lay behind his moods. Because of his work as a minister, there was little money; but Sarah worked to make her home attractive, the children were well

dressed and fed, and she was always well-groomed. Each child was made to feel important in carrying out the daily tasks. Without them doing their part, it would have been impossible to keep the house in any kind of order.

Sarah was to find that her husband had many annoying traits. One of these was his extremely early rising. Even before the farmers would awaken to milk the cows, he would have been up some time, expecting the whole household to join him in Bible reading and prayers by candlelight. Sarah adjusted to his hours.

Jonathan was hardly ever on time for meals and even when he did join the family, he would suddenly get up and return to his studies and writing. However, each night he gave one full hour of completely undivided attention to his children; listening to their needs and praying with them. Perhaps the greatest memory they had of their parents was to see the love and respect their father and mother had for each other.

History shows the heritage of this uncommon union was to be responsible for in succeeding generations: 350 ministers, a Vice President of the United States, governors of three states, controller of the U.S. Treasury, mayors of three cities, thirteen college presidents, 100 lawyers, sixty-five professors, sixty-six physicians, thirty judges, etc.[1]

I can think of another example of a godly marriage even stronger than the one described above. Let me profile their union and see if you can guess whom I am describing.

Strong feelings for her marked their relationship from the beginning. In fact, there never was anyone else for whom he really cared. But because he was older, from the start his love showed itself most in the unselfish way he committed himself to her happiness and well-being. It was his great desire that she should become all God intended her to be, and in no way would he inhibit this from happening—just the opposite was true. So completely did he give himself to this end that eventually it resulted in his death.

Understanding fully what he was about to do, he gave no hint of having sensed that it was a mistake. Close associates who knew him well would say, "Given a second chance, he would have done it the same way again, for he loved her as he loved himself!" Her great contribution to the world in years to come would prove his faith in her to be valid.

If love for her was his outstanding quality, hers for him was respect. Always she admired him, believed and trusted in him, and was proud to be his bride. In spite of his attention, she never allowed herself to view her role as being quite as noteworthy as his. In her mind, he was the one deserving honor and praise, and often she was the first to express it. Careful not to ridicule him or in any way talk slightingly, she instead spoke his name reverently. Seldom did she take his love for her for granted. Instead, she returned it as best she could and sought by her actions to make him very happy.

In decisions she submitted to him when the occasion called for it. And even after his tragic death, she continued to make choices on the basis of what she felt would please him most. Sometimes, in fact, keeping his memory alive cost her dearly in one way or another. But she didn't complain, for it was he who gave her life meaning.

Love and respect for one another marked these two, even as it would later mark Jonathan and Sarah Edwards—but then the latter couple was actually emulating the couple I've been describing. This model, of course, is Christ and the church, his true love.

"Husbands, love your wives, just as Christ loved the church and gave himself up for her to make her holy, cleansing her by the washing with water through the word, and to present her to himself as a radiant church, without stain or wrinkle or any other blemish, but holy and blameless. In this same way, husbands ought to love their wives as their own bodies."

"Wives, submit to your husbands as to the Lord . . . as the church submits to Christ, so also wives should submit to their husbands in everything."

Christian couples should emulate the relationship of Christ and his true church. That understanding is the beginning of true spirituality for married people everywhere.

NOTES

1. Joan Brown, *Wings of Joy* (Old Tappan, N.J.: Fleming H. Revell, 1977), pp. 107-108.

9

Karen

A Tribute to Marriage

More than a quarter of a century ago, at eight o'clock in the evening, in my home church in Wheaton, Illinois, my husband and I were wed.

Most of the tales of our wedding day have now passed into the realm of family lore, stories we laugh about. But they were real enough that I often whispered in my daughter's ear, "Oh, you don't want a big church wedding, do you? Have a small, private celebration. Or better yet—why don't you just elope?"

Actually, I think this was part of the source of my wedding- day problems. My mother wanted a big church wedding and I wanted a small, unassuming private one. So we compromised . . . and had a big church wedding!

Now, this in itself isn't so unusual. Many a young bride has been wed in the same kind of traditional affair with friends and family in attendance. But the difficulty that complicated these grand plans for us was that my family never spent any money for anything we didn't have to. We prided ourselves on traveling through life as thriftily as possible. Actually, this meant that nothing was ever hired out; we did all tasks from household repairs to weddings by ourselves.

Take my wedding dress, for example. I had vowed that my Gram, an accomplished seamstress, was not going to wear herself out sewing my wedding dress. Fortunately, I was able to find a sample dress—the kind wedding shops have for prospective brides to try on in order to see which styles they prefer—made of beautiful lace and satin for only thirty dollars.

Never mind that the bodice was two sizes too large and needed alteration. Never mind that the hem was several inches too long and there were some thirty yards of fabric in the three layers of the skirt. Never mind that my little Gram, on her hands and knees, painstakingly hand-stitched every inch. I should have begun suspecting something was amiss in our approach when one day I heard her sigh, "Do you know, Karen Sue, I think it would have been easier to make you a dress from scratch."

And then there was the wedding cake which an acquaintance was engaged to bake and decorate for a reasonably low fee. The only problem was that she didn't provide delivery service. My future father-in-law and my husband-to-be were forced to struggle with that gargantuan mountain of flour and sugar and frosting in the back seat of their station wagon. It poured rain the afternoon before my wedding, the cake slipped, and Dad hollered, "Catch the cake, David!" Although disaster was averted, David discovered there was no convenient way to steady a wobbling wedding cake.

I slept on the living room couch the night before my wedding day because the house was full of my father's family, and my dad would never have thought of housing kin in a motel. We needed all available space for great-aunts and grand-uncles.

David was up until three in the morning the night

before our wedding, finishing his work in order to take a four-day honeymoon. He was kept so busy running errands for my mother and attending rehearsals and rehearsal dinners that he didn't have time for a fresh shave even for his own wedding.

The day of the wedding I had to go out into the rainstormy afternoon to pick blossoms from the mock orange bushes so my little cousins could scatter petals on the aisle during the wedding march, and humidity always ruins my hairdo. Daddy stepped on my wedding gown as we were rounding the back pews, and the photographer took so long after the ceremony that by the time he was finished, most of the wedding guests were gone.

Then some of the young men with whom we worked took all the tires off our car, which we thought we had successfully hidden, and while we were waiting for a good friend to put the tires back on our car these same young men came cheekily into our living room with the intention of kidnaping me. But my wonderful new brother-in-law let the air out of their tires and David and I made a successful getaway, unmolested.

We spent the four days of our honeymoon in a far-from- luxurious cabin in the woods, rented from friends, and David and I worked our heads off getting ready for the next two weeks, a Bible conference where we were in charge of the children's program. We were responsible for two hundred children from babes-in-arms to junior highers for two hours a day for fourteen days. Our superiors must have liked the job that we did, for they invited us to take the same responsibility the next year.

I have been married for over a quarter of a century, and as I look back on that string of humorous and not-so-humorous events, I realize that the whole confusing spectacle of ceremony and exhausting pressure were strangely prophetic. These very things are what the years of my life with this man, David Mains, have been like.

A Key Element Of Healthy Families

Dolores Curran, the author of *Traits of a Healthy Family*, makes an important point in listing fifteen traits that professionals believe are essential to a healthy family life: ***The healthy family exhibits an unusual relationship between the parents.*** She quotes one of her resource experts, an administrator in an accredited family program: "The healthiest families I know are the ones in which the mother and father have a strong, loving relationship between themselves. This seems to flow over to the children and even beyond the home. The strong primary relationship seems to breed security in the children, and, in turn, fosters the ability to take risks, to reach out to others, to search for their own answers, become independent, and develop a good self- image."[1]

The same concept applies to the spiritual life: If we want our children to be spiritually healthy, we as parents must become spiritually healthy.

1. Dolores Curran, *Traits of a Healthy Family*, (New York: Winston Press, 1983), pp. 39-40.

There has been much hard work. There has rarely been enough money. There has certainly been little luxury. We have had to fight and struggle and "do ourselves" all of the dreams which have burned in our hearts and souls. We have always had hundreds of people around when we would have preferred it to be "just us two." Children and deadlines and ministry have threatened to kidnap our attention from each other, and it has often rained on our celebrations.

We have frequently nearly dropped the special cakes of our lives together. We have had to make room for a houseful of extended family, and we have sometimes tripped over each other while walking down the aisles of our days. Rarely have we had time to put our best faces forward. Our garments often have been altered or secondhand. Frequently we have been exhausted beyond our physical and emotional strengths, serving in areas which were sometimes not our first choices. And always we have had to adjust to each other.

But in this quarter century and more, I have learned a wonderful lesson about marriage. A perfect ceremony does not a perfect marriage make. Neither do circumstances determine the quality of the union. The ceremony occurs, then the marriage becomes. A union is made. Circumstances can only touch it, blow around it, bang on it. But the union is made in spite of the circumstances.

Through these years I have also served as a witness at many of the wedding ceremonies where my minister husband has officiated. I love the wedding sermon in which he has told so many young couples, "It is not your love that sustains the marriage, but from now on, the marriage that sustains your love." These words are quoted from a letter written by Dietrich Bonhoeffer.

It was only recently while reading *Dietrich Bonhoeffer: Letters and Papers from Prison* that I discovered this German theologian wrote these thoughts from his prison cell. They were addressed to his best friend, Eberhard Bethge, who was marrying into the Bonhoeffer family, an occasion of deep joy for Bonhoeffer. But due to the circumstances—the Second World War raging around them, the terrible complications of the Nazi regime in German society, and Bonhoeffer's unjust imprisonment which was eventually to result in his execution—this letter takes on added dimensions.

"Marriage is more than your love for each other,"

Bonhoeffer wrote. "It has a higher dignity and power . . . Your love is your own private possession, but marriage is more than something personal—it is a status, an office. Just as it is the crown, and not merely the will to rule, that makes the king, so it is marriage and not merely your love for each other that joins you together in the sight of God and man. . . ."[1]

Through these years of marriage, I have become convinced of the sanctity of the office of marriage. In a day where so many couples write their own vows, a custom which has lovely aspects, still I am grateful that David and I spoke the old words, the traditional ones which have been whispered and stammered and pronounced by generations and generations before me and which will probably be used by generations and generations to come. "To thee only will I cling . . . in sickness and in health . . . till death do us part."

Marriage is a symbol for the love Christ gives his church. It is a sacrament, a means by which God conveys to the world his intention of how individuals are to love each other, how society is meant to love, how the members of the kingdom of God in heaven are even now loving each other. And that spiritual love is what has sustained our relationship; it is the rock at the very core of this marriage which has lasted despite everything.

I have been married for over a quarter of a century, and I have learned through these years that circumstances do not make the marriage. It is the inward quality of commitment which David and I vowed to each other that hot June evening, with candles flickering in the sanctuary and ferns banking the altar, which has sustained our relationship. It is the vow which we renew each day of our life to live together still, to work together still, to help each other become all God intended for us to become, to advance the cause of the Kingdom of Christ, and to teach each other through our union how to love God, and to teach the offspring of this union how to do the same. This is what makes or breaks a marriage—not the circumstances which blow and bluster around it.

I would like to pay a tribute to marriage. I would like to say that it is possible for a man and woman very different from one another in temperament and style to love each other more a half century after they have repeated their marriage vows than when they were young and fresh and had no idea what life would demand of them.

In this world we need to hear these words: "Love can grow and last!" We need to say them. We need to live them.

And as I give a tribute to marriage, I must also give tribute to the One who has been at the center of the union, to Christ. Without him . . . who knows? Who knows?

He is the One who has given us love enough.

He is the One who has made the living rich.

It is his example that has taught us how to lead and how to be led. Spiritual leadership begins and ends by imitating him.

A tribute to marriage? Most certainly, yes. But most of all, to Christ who has made the marriage last.

NOTES

1. Dietrich Bonhoeffer, *Letters and Papers from Prison*, (New York: Macmillan, 1972).

Couples' Discussion Questions

Take an opportunity—sitting over coffee, in the moments after a meal and before evening activities, or driving somewhere together in a car—to discuss the following questions.

1. How, without words, can we observe the practice of spirituality in one another?
2. What do our activities say about our spiritual priorities?
3. Are there adjustments we need to make in our spiritual goals?

10
Dialogues:
What Does Spiritual Leadership Look Like?

The team of Mains and Mains has had plenty of reason to communicate over the nearly three decades of our marriage. The following dialogues are the result of some of the issues we have faced.

We are convinced that modeling is an excellent way to teach, and while we admit these glimpses into our communication system are the end product rather than the laborious process, we believe that, even in a finished stage, these can be helpful tools for those who need to "see how it is done."

One way to use these dialogues is for husband and wife to read them to each other. We suggest the husband read David's lines and the wife read Karen's. At those points where either of you have questions or where a helpful observation might be made, stop your reading and discuss how the material might assist you. When you're through discussing that point, continue reading.

All the dialogues are short and practical. We suggest you interact with the material using whatever format is best suited to your own situation.

Happy discussions!

I Can Pick You Up When You Fall

KAREN: One of my favorite books is titled *The Second Coming* by Walker Percy. It's a love story about a middle-aged widower who suffers from a physical condition that makes him constantly fall down. He meets a twenty-year-old mental health patient who can't remember things after escaping from confinement where she received shock treatments.

DAVID: Didn't they meet in a greenhouse or something?

KAREN: Well, actually, the widower fell down a hill into the greenhouse where the patient was hiding.

DAVID: Sounds like an unlikely pair. Why do you like this story so much?

KAREN: I particularly love the words she says to him when she realizes they've fallen in love: "I can pick you up when you fall, and you can remember for me when I forget." Those must be some of the most tender words in all literature.

DAVID: "I can pick you up when you fall, and you can remember for me when I forget"?

KAREN: That captures it completely! Just think how many times you've said to me during moments of stress, "Don't worry about that. I've got it covered." Any good marriage is based on all kinds of mutual compensations, and many times you compensate for some weak area in my life that is proving troublesome at a rough moment in our family routine.

DAVID: Like balancing your checkbook for you?

KAREN: Watch it! I'm definitely sensitive to the fact that at my age, I can't make my monthly bank statement balance.

DAVID: Sorry I hit that tender spot, but, after all, am I not just "remembering for you when you forget"?

KAREN: That's right. Partners in a good marriage develop a sensitivity toward one another that allows for this beautiful rhythm of "picking up and remembering." For instance, when you have an enormous work load, I often put aside my own work to give you a hand until your deadlines are past. And many's the time you've pushed a vacuum cleaner, pitched in with dishes, and run out for short-order dinners when my writing schedule became tight.

DAVID: "I can pick you up when you fall, and you can remember for me when I forget." It sounds a lot like the scriptural injunction from the second verse in the sixth chapter of Paul's letter to the Galatians: "Carry each other's burdens, and in this way you will fulfill the law of Christ."

KAREN: That's exactly what it is! No marriage can develop maturity without this loving, sensitive system of mutual compensation.

DAVID: Most good ideas have a shadow side. What if one partner is always compensating and the other is always being compensated for?

KAREN: Good question. There's no mutuality in that relationship. That is not bearing one another's burdens; that is self-centeredness, and sooner or later the partner who is doing most of the "picking up" is going to become resentful. I see mutual compensation like a lovely, stately marriage dance with intricate and gentle movements. I lay down my desires when you have a need, and you do the same for me. And I suppose if you "fall" too long in a specific area, I should quit "dancing" for a while until you learn the right step.

DAVID: In other words, if one partner keeps compensating for the other in an area of need, adult responsibility for personal growth may be delayed. What do you think about taking another go at balancing your checkbook?

KAREN: I was afraid it would come to this . . .

DAVID: Part of healthy, mutual compensation has to include recognizing when your partner is in need.

KAREN: Absolutely! So many times we've said to each other, "This is not the time to tackle that or to talk about this," because of the overload one of us was carrying. We've had to learn to be sensitive during stressful periods, when too much work piled up, when the children had a run of seasonal school activities, or when circumstances threatened which were out of our control.

DAVID: Along these lines, we've learned that when one of us is traveling, the other needs to arrange a schedule which avoids business trips in order to keep the home fires burning. We've learned that times of fatigue or illness are not times for heavy discussions on issues that can be discussed later.

KAREN: We've learned to provide laughter for each other when discouragement sets in, and we've learned to give each other a firm kick in the pants if that was needed. We've learned which trigger words to avoid out of respect for the other's vulnerable areas.

DAVID: In short, we actually are still learning to bear each other's burdens; consequently, we enjoy the fruits of healthy, mutual compensations. By the way, thank you for putting this chapter together, Karen. I ran out of time.

KAREN: Don't mention it. It was my pleasure. I can pick you up when you fall, and you can remember for me when I forget.

DAVID: We'll do your checkbook tomorrow . . .

Helping Your Spouse Handle Criticism

DAVID: Sometimes, married couples get to feeling like the words of that song, "You and me against the world."

KAREN: Particularly when two people have to help each other stand against the winds of criticism.

DAVID: We certainly have had to deal with this problem. During our thirteen years in the local church as pastor and wife, we've learned that one of the major difficulties is handling criticism.

KAREN: That's right. If each church member in a congregation of five hundred criticizes you only once a year, the results become cumulative even if everyone is basically positive about your ministry. A writer friend of mine recently said that it takes seventeen "strokes" to make up for one blow!

DAVID: And now we're working in a daily radio ministry with a national audience. Our "congregation" is in the millions, and while most of the mail that comes into our office is positive, we still receive a great deal of severe and unkind criticism—real blows!

KAREN: Like the letter which suggested to our founder that he close down the broadcast rather than allow it to disintegrate under the leadership of David Mains.

DAVID: Or the letter which criticized your laughter on the broadcast, saying "Saving souls is no laughing matter!"

KAREN: That didn't bother me so much as the one that complained about my "Little-Bo-Peep voice."

DAVID: All right, enough of this wound-licking. Criticism is part of the fabric of life. It comes from friends, enemies, family, employers, employees. One of the supports that married partners can give each other is to help each other deal with criticism.

KAREN: Do you mean developing a siege mentality, a "you and me against the world" outlook?

DAVID: No, I mean helping each other decide which criticism is valid, or which *part* of which criticism is valid, and what can be legitimately ignored.

KAREN: Necessity has made us pretty good at this, hasn't it? In the pastorate, I learned not to accept third-hand criticism. "So-and-so said such-and-such" is not worth my grief. Most often, the words are reported out of context and reflect unexpressed feelings of the reporter who doesn't have courage enough to deal with me up-front in a first-hand kind of exchange.

DAVID: And I have learned not to worry about general comments like, "You know, you're a lousy speaker." Those I generally discard. But I can work on specific suggestions. A member of our radio audience recently challenged me about my habit of splitting infinitives. Specific items like this can be evaluated and acted on if necessary.

KAREN: We can also help each other to identify a pattern in the criticism.

DAVID: And sometimes spouses are the only ones with enough of a long-range view to help. For instance, a spouse has been around long enough to know that Mother used to comment on a certain peculiarity, the children still complain about it, and on the last annual review, the boss suggested that correcting it would create better work relationships. That's a pattern.

KAREN: Spouses can help one another be thin-skinned about criticism rather than thick-skinned.

DAVID: By "thin-skinned" I presume you mean striving for an attitude that says, "There's probably some truth here somewhere"?

KAREN: That's right. Proverbs 10:17 says, "He who heeds discipline shows the way to life, but whoever ignores correction leads others astray."

DAVID: The attitude we attempt to achieve is one which listens to the reproof, even when it has been delivered in an unloving manner. Then we go to prayer and ask, "Lord, is there anything in this criticism that might be valid?" Then we listen. Sometimes the Holy Spirit indicates the criticism was unfair—and that's wonderful. But just as often, we hear the Holy Spirit say, "So glad you brought this up. There's something I've been meaning to talk over with you."

KAREN: And the ways the Holy Spirit verifies the criticism can be through a Scripture passage which convicts us, through the tongue of another person totally removed from the source of the first criticism, or even through a sermon.

DAVID: Or even through a loving spouse . . .

KAREN: So glad you brought that up. That reminds me— there's something *I've* been meaning to talk to you about.

Healthy Battlefields for Marital Wars

DAVID: The topic for this dialogue is a subject with which we have a wealth of experience.

KAREN: You mean arguments in marriage . . .

DAVID: That's right, and yet the interesting thing about arguments in our marriage is that they have grown less and less through the years, even though our responsibilities and pressures have grown more and more.

KAREN: The ones we do have are productive, not just an endless repetition of old wars that lead to marital battle fatigue.

DAVID: One of the reasons for this is that we have learned how to wage fair fights. We laid down some healthy battlefield rules.

KAREN: And the basic truth we have discovered is that mature Christian couples can be in control of the arguments rather than the arguments being in control of them.

DAVID: The first healthy battlefield rule is: Choose the optimum terrain over which to fight.

KAREN: I have been saved many a war wound by your words, "Karen, go to bed. We'll talk about it in the morning." I wasn't spoiling for a fight; you knew I just desperately needed R & R.

DAVID: Don't fight when there is exhaustion, unusual stress, or deep emotional pain. I remember a pastoral intern who was upset by some things you said to me . . .

KAREN: Don't you mean some *nasty* things I said to you?

DAVID: I explained to him that you were emotionally distraught and needed to get it out. We'd pick up the conversation when there wasn't so much emotional strain. You've done the same for me.

KAREN: Particularly after church board meetings! Every marriage needs to provide room for the parties to vent without those ventilation sessions leading to arguments.

DAVID: Another battlefield rule is to insist on balance in the heated exchange. Each party must say what he or she feels, and each must hear what the other is saying.

KAREN: We have friends who argue by sitting in chairs with their backs to each other. This way they are forced to listen to what each other is saying as well as to express clearly what they are saying.

DAVID: Balance means equal amounts of expression. It means saying to your partner, "Now, I've been doing the talking. I want to hear what you are thinking and feeling."

KAREN: Another technique we've developed in striking a balance is to ask, "What did you just hear me say?"

DAVID: Then the listening party will repeat back what was heard. The listener might also start this exchange by saying, "Stop a moment and let me tell you what I just heard. Did I hear you say what you wanted me to hear?" In the middle of the heatedness, there is a communicative rationality at work.

KAREN: Another rule is to draw fences around the battlefield. Agree with one another that there are certain boundaries you will not cross. We refuse to open old wounds or drag out mistakes from years gone by.

DAVID: Certainly not! If we're going to fight, let's have fresh fights. Another fence we refuse to cross is not to hit one another in vulnerable ego areas . . .

KAREN: Like my not being able to keep an orderly checkbook and being frequently overdrawn.

DAVID: Yes, and like my touchiness about being overweight. Vulnerable ego areas need compassionate hands, not the drawn swords of marital frays.

KAREN: The last healthy battlefield rule is to allow ourselves creative options for solving our problems.

DAVID: That's right. Together we have discarded the old need to win. We have moved our marital arguments away from the hackneyed "I'm right/you're wrong" scenario. Now in our discussions, we seek to discover how we can help one another overcome in this area where there seems to be so much conflict.

KAREN: So if you're going to fight, choose the optimum battlefield.

DAVID: Strike a balance between expression and listening.

KARAN: Set up fences beyond which you both agree not to go.

DAVID: Find creative solutions. Forget the win-lose/right- wrong approach to marital arguments.

KAREN: Then perhaps you'll discover, along with us, that marital conflict can be productive.

DAVID: With healthy battlefield rules, you may find you're fighting less and enjoying it more!

What in the World Is Mental Fidelity?

DAVID: Karen, you and I have discovered a sure key for successful marriage. If we could market the idea, we'd be wealthy!

KAREN: What do you mean, David? We *are* wealthy. Even though we can't make a financial profit on this key to a successful marriage, we have profited from it ourselves because we practice this idea. It has made us emotionally rich.

DAVID: This idea was introduced years ago by Christ. He said, "You have heard that it was said, 'Do not commit adultery.' But I tell you that anyone who looks at a woman lustfully has already committed adultery with her in his heart" (Matthew 5:27- 28).

KAREN: The key for successful marriage that we are talking about is *mental fidelity*.

DAVID: Right! This custom is rarely practiced in our culture, but it means that we pledge ourselves not only to be faithful with our bodies but to be faithful with our minds as well.

KAREN: This practice of mental fidelity demands disciplining our minds to be faithful. We promise not to fantasize about members of the opposite sex, nor to think about what it would be like to make love or to go to bed with them. We don't allow ourselves to spend time dreaming in a romantic way of any others besides our mate.

DAVID: I think some people may be saying, "That's too high a price to pay for a successful marriage."

KAREN: Or they may be thinking, "You dreamers! Mental fidelity is impossible!"

DAVID: We are not saying this idea is easy. It is *not* easy, particularly in our culture where everything we read and view proclaims that the extra-marital affair—of the body or of the mind—is perfectly permissible, even desirable.

KAREN: Mental fidelity is possible, however, and we are living proof of the fact that a married couple can practice this discipline.

DAVID: This has come through almost thirty years of marriage because of much determination. It starts with behavior or attitudinal modification. If I find myself tempted to think of another woman lustfully, I have learned to refuse that temptation by saying to myself, "I have vowed to be faithful to Karen in my mind as well as with my body. I am determined to focus all my romantic thoughts toward my wife."

KAREN: Mental fidelity has been enhanced for us by removing those stimulants that would turn our minds from one another. Many women make a regular habit of watching the daytime soaps where the plots center on a variety of forms of sexual promiscuity. They need to turn away from the television set in order to strengthen their vow of "to thee only will I cling."

DAVID: I remember years ago when I first looked at a *Playboy* magazine. I realized then that I could not handle that whole philosophy of sexual hedonism, and I made a vow that for the sake of our marriage I would never look at another—and I haven't!

KAREN: Thank you. Each individual will have to examine areas in his or her life which decrease mental fidelity and decide what he or she can do to begin the discipline of attitude modification. We believe mental fidelity, as difficult as it is, is the correct Christian posture.

DAVID: As far as mental fidelity being too high a price to pay for a happy marriage, we have found the results of years of practice to be well worth the discipline.

KAREN: There is a deep sense of trust, a well of peace at the center of our relationship that comes from the fact that I know the commitment of David's romantic mind is for me alone.

DAVID: And the mutuality of both partners resting in this security frees our creative energies to do the work of God we have been given to do in this world.

KAREN: It also, amazingly, frees us to relate to the opposite sex in a Christlike way. Because David has learned to focus his romantic intentions toward me, it has freed him to be a brother and father toward other women in the body of Christ. So many women have said to me, "Your husband is the first man I have ever been able to trust."

DAVID: So this key to successful marriage that we recommend, mental fidelity, is the practice of being faithful to one's mate in mind as well as body.

KAREN: Are you still wishing you had a way to market this idea, David?

DAVID: I guess I just wish I could convince a few people of its benefits. I'd like, most of all, to salvage a great many marriages.

KAREN: If enough couples were convinced of the value of this idea, it might salvage a country as well.

Part Two

Making It Work as Families

11 The Nurture Center

Karen

The writings of Chaim Potok beautifully portray the sub-culture of a devout Jewish community of faith. In the novel *The Chosen*, Potok contrasts two boyhood friends, Danny Saunders and Reuven Malter. Danny was reared in strict, Hasidic Jewry, while Reuven grew up in an Orthodox but less legalistic faith. One scene captures Talmud study on a Sunday afternoon at the home of rabbi Reb Saunders. Reuven narrates the action:

> I realized soon enough that the *Pierkei Avot* text was merely being used as a sort of jumping-off point for them, because they were soon ranging through most of the major tractates of the Talmud again. And it wasn't a quiz or a quiet contest this time, either. It was a pitched battle. . . . Danny caught his father in a misquote, ran to get a Talmud from the shelf, and triumphantly showed his father where he had been wrong.

This intellectual challenge and counter-challenge continues between son and father, with both obviously enjoying themselves. The father glows as he is forced to acquiesce to the younger's rendition of a passage or to his incisive questioning. Reuven continues:

> The battle went on for a long time, and I slowly became aware of the fact that both Danny and his father, during a point they might be making or listening to, would cast inquisitive glances at me, as if to ask what I was doing just sitting there while all this excitement was going on . . .

Reuven finally joins in, joyfully realizing he has the intellect and training to hold his own with the theological combatants.[1]

I wish the spiritual training between all Christian parents and their children could be as dynamic as this moment Potok describes.

In an article titled, "There's Nothing Wrong With Hand-Me- Down Faith," pastor Ray Stedman concentrates on a phrase from Deuteronomy 6, the Old Testament job description for Hebrew parents. The phrase is, ". . . and you shall teach them diligently to your children." (NASB).

Stedman writes, "Notice that *you* shall teach. Like many licenses, this one should be stamped 'non-transferable.' The Sunday School and church cannot substitute for parents in teaching spiritual truth. Only parents have the time, the concern, and the relationship with their children to make it work. No one has as much influence on children as parents. Therefore, God holds parents responsible to teach their children how to love him with all their hearts, and souls, and might."[2]

Stedman is right. The home, the Christian home, is the primary center for the spiritual nurturing of the child. Outside institutions—Christian schools, child evangelism clubs, campus ministries—must always be viewed as supplemental. Sending a child to church two hours every week without making the home the primary center for spiritual nurturing is a little like giving a child a meal once a week and then letting him fend for himself the rest of the time. That is what I call neglect, spiritual neglect.

A Faithless Generation

Dr. Robert Coles, a prominent Harvard psychologist, has said, "Many of the kids I've looked at don't have faith. That's the problem. They don't have religious faith or the kind of religious faith that can be called natural religion as St. Augustine talks about it. They have lost everything except preoccupation with themselves, and this is enhanced every day by the way we are brought up. Child psychiatrists are brought into this because parents are endlessly concerned with what stage of growing up their children are going through. This is faith centered on one's self. It isn't faith in God, in some transcendent belief."

Coles believes that parents have abandoned their moral authority. "Unfortunately," he writes, "a lot of people have lost their faith in God and in our own institutions, our history, our nation. What do they have faith in? They have faith in themselves and what they cultivate in themselves. They have faith in these various newspaper columnists who give advice *ad nauseum*. They have faith in fads and secular authority."[1]

1. Dr. Robert Coles, "What Makes Children Grow Up Good?", *U. S. Catholic*, August 1979.

A ride through the toll booths in the Chicago area reminds me that children are missing. Little faces look woefully from shredded, weather-beaten posters.

"Missing," the block letters read. "Have you seen this child?" Breakfast milk cartons and the backs of trucks proclaim the dismal reality that children in our society are being kidnaped . . . many whose fates are never discovered.

Statistics on missing children are hard to come by, but there are basically four categories: (1) voluntary missing (includes runaways); (2) parental kidnaping; (3) stranger abductions, and; (4) a catch-all "other." Boundaries between the categories tend to blur.

The best estimates are that about one million American youngsters leave home each year, with 90 percent returning in two weeks. That leaves approximately one hundred thousand children unaccounted for. The experts add about twenty-five thousand to one hundred thousand stolen by divorced or separated parents, and suddenly the number becomes alarming.

When a stranger steals a child, anything can happen. Parents of missing children hope that their child will end up in a loving, caring family, perhaps through black-market adoption— but the cruel truth is that a missing child stands a fair chance of being murdered. Each year an estimated twenty-five hundred children in the United States disappear who later are found dead.

Many thousands of others are used for much more calculated reasons. The director of a national child protection agency stated, "Kids are constantly being sought for the lucrative child-prostitution business."

In other words, this nation of liberty now has a major societal menace to deal with. A few years ago there was no centralized agency to monitor the disappearance of children, and local police were extremely reluctant to get into the action.

"Our priorities are mixed up," said a spokesperson quoted in a *Reader's Digest* article. "If someone steals a car, he can be traced and caught because we have a national computer system for tracing stolen cars. But children apparently aren't that important to us."

Finally, in 1984, the National Center for Missing and Exploited Children was established. The center is a clearinghouse of computerized information to aid parents in tracking and locating missing children.

Few people would dispute that it was high time we did something about the plight of these abducted little ones.

Yet strangely enough, the spiritual kidnaping of children by the dark enemy of our souls happens all the time, and many church parents seem almost relaxed about it.

What will raise the consciousness of Christians to the very real possibility that one day their own children will be listed among the missing, among those absent from the list of followers of Christ?

Will imprinted cartons at church suppers do it—"Missing: Have you seen this child?" What about posters on the back of Sunday School buses with the faces of those who have left the Christian cause: "Pray for this missing child"?

Parents need to take early precautions that will do as much as possible to ensure the faith development of their children. We must prevent this snatching away of our most cherished resource.

Parents, your Executive Committee needs to meet regularly to design spiritual ventures and home teaching that will continually lead your children into a love of the Lord. The faith development of your offspring needs to be a priority, the subject of on-going, important discussions that may well lead to necessary changes in lifestyle.

If our children disappear spiritually, we may have to face the fact one day that while we gave them everything they needed materially, we disregarded all their primary spiritual needs. Donald Joy, a professor of human development at Asbury Theological Seminary, says:

> We're so caught up in an age of spiraling affluence that we probably need to underscore the fact that there is no substitute for the parent—a parent who not only lives with the child, but interacts with the child, exercises generosity, fairness, discipline, and all that. To take a second job or feel you're doing the best thing for your family by increasing your income can be very destructive. . . . Some guys ought to resign their traveling jobs and become a parent who is available.[3]

Socrates once said to the people of Athens: "Why do you turn and scrape every stone to gather wealth, and take so little care of your children, to whom one day you must relinquish it all?"

Parents must understand that the Christian home is the primary center for the spiritual nurture of their children.

A few years ago, John H. Westerhoff III started a whole new wave of thinking in Christian education by asking whether there weren't stages of faith development in children comparable to their readily observed physical development. In his book *Will Our Children Have Faith?*, he says, "The structures and programs of the church can only be justified insofar as they enable the community of faith to be an historical agency through which God remakes the human world."

What modern Christian educators seem to be saying is that the church is not the primary institution for the spiritual training of the child. Rather, it is the individual family unit in which that development must occur.

Horace Bushnell wrote a book considered by many to be a high-water mark of Christian education. In *Chris-*

tian Nurture, Bushnell made a statement which at first jarred my evangelical thinking. After considering the statement, however, I think I essentially and ideally agree with him:

> What is the true idea of Christian education? . . . that the child is to grow up a Christian, and never know himself as being otherwise. In other words, the aim, effort and expectation should be, not, as is commonly assumed, that the child is to grow up and sin, to be converted after he comes to a mature age; but that he is to be open on the world as one that is spiritually renewed, not remembering the time when he went through a technical experience.[4]

Conversion? Yes! A moment (or moments) of crucial decision? Yes! But all of these come in the context of a spiritual environment so daily, so constant, that the experiences don't seem to stand out. They do not come in contrast to a poverty of spiritual life, but are integral to a rich and banqueted process.

This can only happen in a Christian home where spirituality is integrated, where the parents joyfully learn new truth about God and apply it to their relationships, to their social concerns, and to their moral and ethical choices. It will only happen in a home where spiritual language—about God, about Scripture, about Christian decision-making, about the reality of Christ's presence—is habitual, natural, delightful.

Westerhoff focuses on four levels of faith development and proposes that everyone needs to go through the initial stages in order to reach the more advanced ones. Those faith plateaus are:

1. *The experiential level.*

This level is childlike (unfortunately, a level many adults never outgrow) in that it adopts the active belief system of others. Westerhoff believes that if children live a rich faith life up to the age of twelve in a home environment where religious ritual, tradition, and story telling are at least as important as doctrine, theology, and content, they will naturally move to the second level of faith upon approaching adolescence.

2. *The affiliative level.*

Here the child acquires a sense of place and of belonging, of community. Campus Bible clubs and youth groups are often important organizations to help those at this stage on their on- going spiritual journey. These organizations are not more important than the home environment, but they are often necessary accessories if faith is to be expressed outside of the individual family context.

3. *The searching level.*

Children at this level test their parents' beliefs, often with peers. They doubt, experiment, and question. Group dialogue is often the best way for this searching level to develop. The family that has built a strong level of integrated daily faith, rather than a sterile religiosity, is much better at weathering this adolescent period (whether it comes during the teens or the early twenties). Many people stay at this level, accepting a social kind of faith rather than one that demands personal spiritual growth. Eventually, however, all who seek true spirituality must enter the final level.

4. *The owned faith.*

Here spirituality is self-directed, chosen because of personal preference, and integrated into everyday living. This is the faith that we as adults and parents should insist upon for ourselves. It is the kind of faith—or perhaps, the groping toward this level—which we should model for our offspring.[5]

When spiritual training happens primarily in the family, when parents understand and take responsibility for the job description outlined for them in Ephesians 6:4 ("... bring [your children] up in the discipline and instruction of the Lord"), then the church becomes an effective supplement to the faith process. It can provide a broader community in which the child can stretch, discuss, observe, find acceptance and security. But it is no substitute for the family.

Bushnell also makes a remarkable statement about the faith community in the broader context:

> True community necessitates the presence and interaction of three generations. Too often the church either lacks the third generation or sets the generation apart. Remember that the third generation is a generation of memory, and without its presence the other two generations are locked into the existential present. While the first generation is potentially the generation of vision, it is not possible to have visions without a memory, and memory is supplied by the third generation. The second generation is the generation of the present. When it is combined with the generations of memory and vision, it functions to confront the community with reality; but left to itself in the present, life becomes intolerable and meaningless. Without interaction between and among the generations, each making its own unique contribution, Christian community is difficult to maintain.[6]

This idea seems to be behind the teaching of Psalm 78:5-7:

> He decreed statues for Jacob and established the law in Israel, which he commanded our forefathers to teach their children, so the next generation would know them, even the children yet to be born, and they in turn would tell their

> children. Then they would put their trust in God and would not forget his deeds but would keep his commands.

In other words, though the primary responsibility for spiritual nurture rests with the parents, they do not have to undertake this enormous task on their own. The community of faith offers a rich resource of memory and of experience. The couple or the single parent can go to the generation beyond them for support, advice, and encouragement. Whether through an extended family, through the leadership of spiritual elders, or in the literature and tradition of church life, help is available.

The Jewish child of the Old and New Testament, reared in a devout home, was enriched by spiritual nourishment. A passage in the Mishnah maps out the stages of life: "At five years of age, reading of the Bible; at ten years, learning the Mishnah; at thirteen years, bound to the commandments; at fifteen years, the study of the Talmud . . ." Six or seven was the age at which a parent in Palestine was legally bound to attend to the schooling of his son.

In addition to this intellectual training, there were daily prayers in the home, morning and evening. There were domestic rites, all with spiritual reasons—the kosher food, the ceremonial washings, the careful choosing of wardrobe. There were family observances of the feasts, the weekly celebration of Sabbath with twenty-six hours set aside as holy, the annual festivals in which even national holidays had religious orientations. Whole systems of mnemonic devices were developed to retain verses of Scripture or benedictions or wise sayings. Anything that would enhance the careful training of memory in spiritual things was developed and used, and it is this which has been one of the continuing mental characteristics of the Jewish people.

On the heels of all this, imagine how worshiping in the temple would add to the rich, daily, spiritual environment of a Jewish child's home . . .

Imagine the courts of Yahweh's house at Jerusalem—the white-marbled, gold-adorned halls under heaven's blue arch. Picture the glorious building with its terraced vistas. Imagine the great throng of white-robed priests, busily moving about the smoke and odor rising from the sacrifice on the altar of burnt offering. Visualize the hushed silence of the multitude, the lifted hands, then all falling down to worship at the time of incense. Think of the priests on the steps that led to the innermost sanctuary, lifting their hands, speaking loudly the words of blessing over the people. Imagine them pouring out the drink offering, the Levites chanting the Psalms, their voices rising and swelling in volume. Try to hear the exquisite treble of children's voices, accompanied by instruments and the threefold blasts from silver trumpets.

Could any child growing up in this twofold atmosphere, where religious life was central to daily life and where weekly worship amplified it, doubt the importance of spirituality?

A child growing up in this sort of environment could not help but absorb spiritual nourishment. His spiritual training was organic to his living. It was integrated in daily life; it wasn't an odd aberration stuck on the backside of the weekly calendar because his parents thought some sort of spiritual training was wise.

We, too, have impressionable children whom an enemy would like to kidnap from the household of faith. Only with rigorous self-examination can we determine if our children are spiritually neglected. As our children grow, hidden spiritual deprivations become all too apparent. And one future day we may ruefully awaken to the terrible truth that our children have become statistics . . .

part of those who are missing from the household of faith.

Many of us have work to do. For God's sake and for the sake of our children, let's get to work!

NOTES

1. Chaim Potok, *The Chosen*, New York: Fawcett Crest, 1967), pp. 155-156.

2. Ray Stedman, "There's Nothing Wrong with Hand-Me-Down Faith," "How to Teach Your Children about God" series, "Chapel of the Air" radio program.

3. Donald Joy, "How to Teach Your Children about God" series, "Chapel of the Air" radio program.

4. Horace Bushnell, *Christian Nurture,* (New Haven: Yale University Press, 1847).

5. John H. Westerhoff III, *Will Our Children Have Faith?* (New York: Seabury Press, 1976).

6. Bushnell, *Christian Nurture*.

Couples' Discussion Questions

1. Whom do I see as the primary source of spiritual training for my child? Myself? Or someone else?
2. What hinders me from performing this vital function in my home?
3. Have I thought about spiritual neglect in the context of eventually having "missing children"?
4. What is the first thing I must do to begin changing (or improving) the spiritual nurture of my child?
5. What are my spouse's best gifts in the spiritual training of our children? What are my own? How can we be the most effective team, working together? What kind of division of labor can we take to make sure the task is done in the best possible manner?

12

David and Karen

Do I Have to Lead Like Everyone Else?

The essential role of the Christian family is to provide a *spiritual* environment in which husband, wife, and any offspring can learn to love God and serve him. This is what makes a Christian family distinctly Christian.

The basic difference between a Christian family and a non-Christian family is that the former is God-centered, attempting to live out a Holy Spirit-led Christlikeness under its own roof and then in the world beyond its doors. It is serious about passing on the faith.

Psalm 78:4-8 talks about this:

> We will tell the next generation
> the praiseworthy deeds of the LORD,
> his power, and the wonders he has done.
> He decreed statutes for Jacob
> and established the law in Israel,
> which he commanded our forefathers
> to teach their children,
> so the next generation would know them,
> even the children yet to be born,
> and they in turn would tell their children.

Then they would put their trust in God
  and would not forget his deeds
  but would keep his commands.
They would not be like their forefathers—
  a stubborn and rebellious generation,
whose hearts were not loyal to God,
  whose spirits were not faithful to him.

Too many Christian parents have not adopted this charge as their own. They think that the Sunday School, the youth group, campus Bible clubs, or Christian schools are going to do it for them. They think these outside forces will inoculate their children (or themselves) with spiritual doses big enough to protect their family from forces hostile to biblical faith.

That is a fairy tale. It will not happen—especially in this society of unbelief.

In earlier generations, society at least gave tacit support to the Judeo-Christian lifestyle. Stores were closed on Sunday. Church attendance was considered important. Moral and ethical absolutes based on scriptural principles were at the core of legal judgments.

No longer. Now individual interpretations of life supersede any absolute moral code. Sexual morality has been jettisoned. Religion is excluded from the classroom. We have shifted from the crucial corporate question, "What is best for the community?" to a self-centered emphasis, "What's best for me?"

Yet the truth is that our secular society—with its media that scoffs at religious belief, its behavioral sciences that promise to help mankind command its own destiny, and its liberalized judicial system—has not been able to deliver.

Religion, true spirituality, is concerned primarily with discovering the deepest meanings of life. It sustains integrity when tested, gives a sense of the reason for being, and builds a moral and ethical allegiance which is good not only for the individual but for the whole.

In this kind of world, it is essential that the Christian family understands and works diligently to establish a spiritual environment.

Once upon a time, most men and women farmed their own land. Organized labor consisted of small groups of blacksmiths, shoemakers, and other craftspeople.

But during the Industrial Revolution, factories and mines needed large numbers of workers, and laborers came in from the farms. Factory and mine owners often ignored the welfare of their employees, so the workers of the 1800s organized labor unions and sought to better their wages and working conditions. Organizers worked for an eight-hour day, the abolition of child labor, safety on the job, and other reforms.

This trend was captured in the historic music of America. "Eight Hours" became the official song of organized labor when a serious campaign for an eight-hour workday began after the Civil War. "We're sure that God has willed it," the song said, "and we mean to have eight hours/ we're summoning our forces/from the shipyard, shop and mill/ eight hours for work/ eight hours for rest/ eight hours for what we will. . . ."[1]

Ever since men and women have been forced to work for others, there has been this lament about the boss. Methods of leadership that worked in one set of circumstances become ineffective and burdensome in another.

Authors John Naisbitt and his wife Patricia Aburdene insist in their book *Re-inventing the Corporation* that the old corporate structures will not work any longer. They believe that corporations of the future must eliminate the old, hierarchical boss structure altogether: "The hierarchical structure where everyone has a superior and everyone has an inferior surely is corrupting of the human spirit—no matter how well it served us during the industrial period."[2]

Scripture seems to have anticipated our changing culture by some two thousand years. Its model for servant leadership in essence is paradoxical, a "complementary contradiction" which has increasing implications for contemporary marriage: "Husbands, love your wives, just as Christ loved the church and gave himself up for her, to make her holy. . . ." The apostle's appeal, as we have said before, is always for those on top—Jew, master, husband—to elevate those of lesser position.

A quote from the leadership training manual of a national real estate organization aptly summarizes this paradox of leadership:

> The heady wine of leadership can send anyone on a disaster trip. The higher the position, the stronger the wine. Beginning leaders must learn to sit on their egos by reminding themselves that leaders are just normal human beings who are supposed to serve their followers and not their own egos. It is not an easy lesson to learn, and as leaders move into more rarefied atmospheres, they must learn it over and over again. The problem is one of balance. Leaders must have strong egos to lead; they must also keep thinking well of themselves so they can maintain their personal confidence and continue to lead. But they must eventually learn to live comfortably with the power that is theirs, or their followers will either hope for a fall or actually create it.[3]

Every election year of recent memory has seemed to evoke a spate of articles, newspaper essays, and media commentaries that decry the lack of leadership in our society.

In truth, our changing times require leadership adaptation not only in government, but at the grass-roots level in the common family. Old structures which worked when constant flexibility was not needed are outmoded today because of mobility and because of shifts in culture and society. We need leadership styles that can effectively respond to these shifts.

Authentic Spiritual Leadership

Chua Wee Hian in his excellent book, *The Making of a Leader*, includes a helpful chart distinguishing between secular and spiritual leadership. It doubles as a good measurement for spiritual leadership in the Christian family. Here is the chart:[1]

Secular Authority	*Servant Authority*
"Lord over"	"Servant among"
Power base	Love/obedience base
Give orders	Under orders
Unwilling to fail	Unafraid/model of transformation
Absolutely necessary	Expendable
Drives like a cowboy	Leads like a shepherd
Needs strength to subject	Finds strength in submission
Authoritarian	Steward of authority
Has gold, makes rules	Follows golden rule
Seeks personal advancement	Seeks to please master
Expects to be served	Expects to serve

1. Chua Wee Hian, *The Making of a Leader* (Downer's Grove, Ill.: InterVarsity Press, 1987), p. 23.

The questions couples ask as we speak in conferences and seminars indicate great confusion on the nature of family leadership. Certainly, our busy divorce courts do not help in creating adequate models. Neither do fathers who, either through workaholism or emotional inadequacies, distance themselves from spouse and offspring.

Although countless, expensive studies have been conducted on the quintessential ingredient of leadership, still we are often confused about its nature. Despite modern research, we sometimes don't know much more than the old, hackneyed definition: "A leader is someone who leads and whom other people follow."

Most often, individuals do not want an answer to the question "What is leadership?" as much as they are trying to discover "Do I have leadership potential?" We have an answer to the second question. While it may be that one might not be considered a leader in the marketplace, every parent has the obligation and scriptural encouragement to be a leader in the home.

The sociological and psychological communities have done a great service in distinguishing different types of leadership styles. One of these, the *Personal Profile System*, develops four general categories of leadership styles and insists there is no "right" or "wrong" style:

- The **D** (dominance) personality tries to shape his/her environment and accomplish results by overcoming opposition.
- The **I** (influence) personality attempts to bring others into alliance in order to accomplish results.
- The **S** (steady) personality cooperates with others to accomplish results.
- The **C** (compliance) personality works with

existing circumstances to promote quality in products or service.[4]

Leadership styles may legitimately range over any of these four categories (or a mix thereof). We are shortsighted if we link one form—the old authoritarian, hierarchical model—with the scriptural concept of male headship.

Tools like the *Personal Profile System* help us to understand both ourselves and the styles of those with whom we work and live. Many new tools are helping us see that there are differing, appropriate styles of leadership.

It may well be that one of the frustrations modern males have with headship is that their particular styles don't fit the old, accepted format. Wives who ask the question, "How can I get my husband to be the spiritual head?" need to examine their own expectations. Perhaps he is already leading, but doing it in his own way.

Though the essential element of leadership can't be distilled like chemicals in a laboratory, further distinctions in style can be made and are helpful in evaluation. Some of these styles are more productive in certain family units than others. Research has identified the following leadership styles:

Autocratic

This style requires a high level of control and is highly directive. The autocratic type has a strong sense of duty and believes that it is his/her responsibility to tell others what to do. The person using this style is usually stern, forceful, intimidating, and dominating.

Authoritative

This style blends the needs of those being led with a lower level of control than the autocratic style. It requires a great deal of give-and-take. Rather than expecting everyone to follow a given set of rules, the authoritative type appreciates the unique gifts, abilities, and stages of development of those under him/her. Authoritative parents expect their children to progress from immature to mature behavior, but with help. This style sets limits rather than non-negotiable rules.

Participative

This style takes the player/coach approach. The leader consults with his followers, invites them to work alongside him/her. The leader sets direction through consensus; participation is used to design the goals of a project and to assign appropriate tasks. The participative leader attempts to make co-workers feel as though they are part of the process so that they take ownership in the finished product. She/he maintains some decision-making control in that the ultimate responsibility still rests in his/her hands.

Democratic

This style depends upon the mandate/decision of the group; all actions are put to the vote. Democratic leaders may suggest certain solutions to problems or goals to be accomplished, but allow associates to make the final decision and then must learn to live with the outcome. This style has the ability to function persuasively.

Laissez-faire

This style is often chosen by those reacting against an autocratic authority from the past. It is a let-live, hang-loose style; work associates have a great deal of control. This leader turns the goal setting and decision making over to others who learn that, if work is going to be accomplished, it is generated from below rather than from above. The laissez-faire style is often found in extremely creative persons, but it can cause chaos from too little control. On the other hand, if co-workers are amenable to this style, they compensate by developing capabilities resulting in mutual interdependence.

That brings up the $64,000 question: Which style works best in parenting?

Let's toss out the two extremes (autocratic and laissez- faire), and say that a combination of any of the middle styles, while they develop differing strengths and weaknesses in offspring, are certainly adequate methods of parenting and leadership.

In her book, *Stress and the Healthy Family*, expert Dolores Curran makes a pertinent point about spouse leadership styles. She notes that most often we follow the internal blueprint of our own parents' leadership style—even when we vow we won't—and that it is a myth that the style of husband and wife must be the same:

> I found a *balance of parenting styles* within the stress-reduced family. Parents don't have to agree on every facet of childrearing and can be very different in their approaches without causing upheaval and stress. . . . Repetitive studies show that each child develops a relationship with each parent rather than developing a single relationship with a set of parents. Therefore, in families with one authoritative and one laissez-faire parent, the child responds to each accordingly. Children may argue and negotiate a decision with a permissive parent while automatically accepting the same decision from the other more authoritative parent. This need not create stress between spouses if each parent is comfortable with his or her relationship with the children and if parents recognize the value of complementary styles of parenting.[5]

Curran reports that great tension is caused among parents with different styles who believe they should be practicing the same style. Stress is caused:

1. when one or both parents expect to provide a single style of leadership in parenting;
2. when parents shift frequently between

styles, not because one is more appropriate to the circumstances than the other, but because of insecurity;

3. when a stepparent accustomed to a single, workable style enters the family;
4. when a changing life stage demands another style than the one previously used;
5. when partners don't have a concept of mutual submission and the ability to blend the other's style with their own.

To complete the discussion of leadership in the family, we must further ask, "What is spiritual leadership?" Chua Wee Hian in his excellent book *The Making of a Leader* asks, "How do we recognize spiritual authority in leaders?"[6]

First, he says, we should recognize a quality of submission to spiritual authority in their own lives—obedience to God, obedience to human authority, obedience to the written Word, to the inner ministry of the Holy Spirit.

Second, we should recognize them because their own authority is tested by men and by the forces of darkness. These tests will reveal whether these leaders' authority is based on true spirituality or on human patronage.

Third, true authority exhibits itself in practical service.

Fourth, we recognize spiritual authority as it is demonstrated by the leader's love and example. "The authority by which the Christian leader leads is not power but love, not force but example, not coercion but reasoned persuasion," Hian says. "Leaders have power, but power is safe only in the hands of those who humble themselves to serve."[7]

Spiritual family management doesn't have to equal reading the Bible every night after supper. In reality it is far greater than one given form, and eventually it should influence the whole personality of your home. Reading the Bible every night after supper is a beautiful and workable approach for many families, but not for all.

Spiritual headship means that the father consciously assumes responsibility for the spiritual well-being of his family and then, jointly with his wife, designs the most suitable means possible through which his children will absorb spiritual truth.

Because of the modern media glut, our family has devised a rating scale by which we evaluate all communication forms. We have decided that television has too many minuses and have chosen not to have a set in our home—a unique approach designed for our unique family based on an underlying principle. Consequently, we have become a family of readers.

Part of our approach to spiritual training has been to provide the children with plenty of good reading material. We regularly keep our eye on advertisements in Christian magazines or the catalogs of Christian publishing houses, then take a trip with the children to a local Christian book dealer. The children are allowed to choose any book, and when they have finished reading it, we ask them to share with us what they liked or didn't like. If your children aren't readers yet, you have the delight of reading the new book together.

This method of reading books is an option for us in which we exercise spiritual leadership. It is one of the many means by which we help to create an atmosphere of spiritual growth in our home.

Samuel Logan Brengle was one of the great leaders of the Salvation Army. His life and ministry touched many lives. This was how he viewed spiritual authority:

> It is not won by promotion but by many prayers and tears. It is attained by confession of sins,

> and much heart searching and humbling before God, by self-surrender, a courageous sacrifice of every idol, a bold, deathless, uncompromising and uncomplaining embracing of the cross, and by an eternal, unfaltering looking unto Jesus crucified. It is not gained by seeking great things for ourselves, but rather like Paul, by counting those things that are gain to us as loss for Christ. That is a great price, but it must be unflinchingly paid by him or by her who would not be merely a nominal but a real spiritual leader of people, a leader whose power is recognized and felt in heaven, on earth and in hell.[8]

Most of us will never be looked to by the corporate church as great spiritual leaders; but all of us have the potential, in our own homes, to be viewed by spouse and offspring as someone who demonstrated Christlikeness.

We must say "Yes!" to leadership in our own homes. We must come to terms with our own style; then we must prayerfully vow in our hearts to be the kind of spiritual leaders, at least in our individual families, "whose power is recognized and felt in heaven, on earth and in hell."

NOTES

1. J. Jones and I. G. Blanchard, "Eight Hours," on *The Sounds of History* (New York: Time, Inc., 1964), Record 7.
2. John Naisbitt and Patricia Aburdene, *Re-inventing the Corporation,* (New York: Warner Books, 1985), p. 49.
3. From the personal records and notes of Karen Mains.
4. J. G. Geier, *Personal Profile System* (Performax Systems International, Inc., U.S.A., 1986), p. 7.
5. Dolores Curran, *Stress and the Healthy Family,* (Minneapolis: Winston Press, 1985), pp. 118-123.
6. Chua Wee Hian, *The Making of a Leader,* (Downer's Grove, Ill.: Inter-Varsity Press, 1987), pp. 103-107.
7. Ibid.
8. Ibid., p. 107.

Couples' Discussion Questions

For those couples desiring to become Christlike in their leadership of the home, author Hian includes a helpful list of Jesus' leadership example. He explains that our Lord was a master trainer who understood the advantage of modeling. This list is invaluable for us all, but particularly for those who have had inadequate human models. Read through the following list.

1. Christ called and chose his disciples.
2. He spent time with them.
3. He taught them.
4. He revealed himself to them.
5. He assigned them practical tests.
6. He evaluated their work.
7. He rebuked them when they were in error or mistaken.
8. He prayed for them.
9. He commissioned them to do the task.
10. He left them.

Now discuss: What was good about Christ's model of training/leadership? What implications does this have for our relationship as spouses? What implications does this have for our role as parents?

13 Teach Them before They're Born

David and Karen

Donald Barnhouse once was asked, "At what age can a child understand what it means to love God?"

"You begin teaching a child about God twenty years before he's born," he replied.

Barnhouse meant that a child's initial instruction about God grows out of the character of the parent. The simple truth which each one of us as parents must understand is this: We cannot give to our children a spiritual life which we ourselves do not possess.

A special report of the *Christianity Today Institute* focusing on the spiritual training of children included this comment by Wes Willis, vice-president of a major Sunday School curriculum house: "The healthy Christian development of a child is tied to the continuing development of the parent."

In that same report, Donald Joy, professor of Human Development and Christian Education at Asbury Theological Seminary, said, "Fathers and mothers, just in the business of doing their parenting, are unwittingly the first curriculum for representing God."

The chilling truth and the remarkable opportunity is that parents will model, either negatively or positively, what God is like for their children.

If we are not modeling God in a positive way, it won't matter what we say. With unerring instinct, our children will eventually sense the incongruity of our lives. A child invariably projects our behavior, good or bad, onto his perception of God.

Another Christian educator illustrated this from his own life:

> Through my growing up and even into adulthood, I have found it very easy to accept God as omnipotent, omniscient—a transcendent Being. But it's been much more difficult for me to perceive of a loving, accepting, gracious God. I perceived my father as being aloof, distant, authoritarian; and I never saw any sensitivity or intimacy expressed at all. The intimacy of prayer was foreign to me, because I didn't have that with my father.[1]

If we as parents don't model a personal, lively experience with the Christian disciplines, we have no right to expect our children to develop a prayer life, read the Bible, or to progress in the walk of faith.

If we approach our children with conditional kinds of love, loving them only when they behave in a way that pleases us or when they perform to our high expectations, they will have trouble experiencing God's unconditional love. They will have a hard time believing that though God disciplines us when we misbehave, he never withdraws his love from us. They will struggle as adults to experientially know that God's love is everlasting, from generation to generation.

Child development experts have discovered that 90 percent of the behavioral skills that we take into our adult years are learned, not because of what we have been told to do, but by what we have been shown. In other words, we have learned communication skills, nurturing patterns, ways to demonstrate love, through someone else's example. These abilities were modeled for us, and they were modeled either negatively or positively.

David Thomas, a professor of adult Christian community development at Regis College, described an experience out of his own past:

> My father was not overtly religious. His religion was something very private. Our family would pray together at certain times, but Dad would rarely join us. And that was always a big problem for me. But I remember one day walking through the house and just happening to look into my parents' bedroom. There was my father kneeling alongside the bed praying. You could have knocked me over with a feather! This was a dimension of him I never knew existed.
>
> What I take from that as a general principle is that parents are always on display, always being watched in different ways; and a child will have a pretty good sense of what's authentic and what's not. Certain things done because you say, "We have to do it this way," or "This is the way it's always been done," don't have nearly as much power as the situation where somebody does something unplanned."[2]

Christian parents must become convinced that they cannot give their children a spiritual life they themselves do not have. They must begin to grow spiritually themselves in order to impart a lively faith to their offspring. It's imperative that children sense their parents' religion isn't just a part of what they do for the sake of the child, but that they do it for their own sake, for their own very real and pressing adult needs.

Indifference in Odd Places

Evangelicals expect society at large to ignore spiritual realities. But consider a study recently conducted by the Search Institute in cooperation with thirteen denominations or organizations specializing in youth work.

The study focused on young adolescents and their parents and discovered that, as would be expected, most parents in the study were involved in church. Yet, although institutional religious participation was the norm, religion was not commonly talked about at home. Adolescents were asked, "How often does your family sit down and talk about God, the Bible, or other religious things?" Some 41 to 46 percent of fifth to ninth graders responded "never"; some 29 to 32 percent of the same age group responded "once or twice a month."

When Christ's spiritual authority was challenged, he said, "Do not believe me unless I do what my Father does" (John 10:37).

I wonder how many of us would have the confidence to say that to our own children?

A parent's sign of authority is the same as Christ's. Like him, we must practice what we preach. We must become convinced that what we model is more powerful than what we say.

According to the prophet Moses, a child's spiritual growth began with the parent's spiritual growth. He commanded Hebrew parents to teach the laws of God to their children: "These are the commands, decrees and laws the LORD your God directed me to teach *you* to observe . . . so that *you*, your children and their children after them may fear the LORD your God" (Deuteronomy 6:1, 2).

The summer of our twenty-fifth wedding anniversary, we piled three of our children into the station wagon and drove across the Canadian Rockies on a mad dash cross-continent to reach Vancouver, British Columbia. We timed our arrival to meet an airplane landing with our eldest son on board. Our destination was the World's Fair, followed by a family vacation on the Oregon coastline.

We saw the adventure as an important time to gather the clan, not only to celebrate with us a quarter century of married life, but because we realized it was probably the last time we would be able to gather in this fashion. The original Mains's nuclear unit was about to progress to the next stage: Full-time jobs, new spouses, grandchildren, that coming plateau of extended family.

Our children's ages at the time included one young adult just out of college, one daughter in college, and two sons in high school. After an enjoyable time at the World's Fair, we motored to the Oregon coastline where David and I had been invited to speak at a Bible conference center. The kids took advantage of the beach and spent time sightseeing in the quaint coastal towns.

At one of the meals in the conference center dining hall, a woman with young children leaned over the table to ask what we had done to train our children spiritually. Because Melissa and Joel were sitting with us, we encouraged her to ask them. She did.

"Now that I have two of the Mains children captive," she said, "I want to ask: What did your parents do to train you spiritually?"

We don't believe she was expecting the answers they gave—unplanned, undiscussed, and uncoached by ourselves. We have a feeling she was hoping for tips on family devotions, prayers around the breakfast table, Bible memorization work, stories about being in church morning, noon, and night. We suspect she was looking for a master plan.

"Well, they didn't actually have a rigid plan for us. They didn't really *make* us do anything," our twenty-one-year-old daughter Melissa and our seventeen-year-old son Joel answered in tandem.

"They respected our individuality, encouraged our creativity."

"But they modeled. They had a spiritual life which we observed. And because we saw it and because it was attractive, we wanted it too."

Spontaneous, on-the-spot moments like these are wonderful verifications of everything David and I have strived to achieve in the spiritual training of our children. And it came from the mouths of those who are no longer babes.

I have come to the conclusion that the best way I can improve my children's spiritual lives is to continually improve my own.

And I'm sure that's true of you, too.

NOTES

1. "How to Teach Your Child about God" series, "Chapel of the Air" radio program.
2. David Thomas, "How to Teach Your Child about God" series, "Chapel of the Air" radio program.

Couples' Discussion Questions

Take some time to meditate over the following questions. Then discuss with your spouse how each of you plan to act upon your evaluation.

1. Where am I growing spiritually? Am I growing spiritually?
2. Do my children ever see me praying? Do they pass my door, for instance, and see me on my knees?
3. On a scale of 1-10, with ten being the highest, how do I rate my own spiritual maturity?
4. Which do I do the most, model the Christian life or lecture my children on how they are to model the Christian life?
5. Do I really mean what I say, or am I saying things only because I think a Christian parent should say them?
6. Do I have a specific plan for the near days ahead that will stimulate my own spiritual growth?

14 Spiritual Composting

Karen

I am a frustrated gardener. Gardening provides emotional solace as well as physical exercise for me, but I am continually unable to follow up through the summer on my annual spring vows and good intentions. The compost bin was a good example.

One young man, a friend of my children, built me a long-awaited compost bin as thanks for living with us for a school year. But by the end of the winter freezes, the sides had collapsed. As usual, the story of my material life: One step forward, several steps backward.

It was also symbolic of my entire gardening adventure. Vegetables didn't get planted, but weeds proliferated. Kitchen herbs withered from neglect, and scarcely a rose bush survived competition with an intensive writing schedule.

After the boys had moved the compost bin to a more compatible location (one in which the posts could be sunk into cement), I pulled *The Self-Sufficient Gardener* off my bookshelves and thought, *Oh well, at least we have plenty of green matter*. I had in mind all those weeds which had invaded my land, threatening it with total occupation.

"What was that recipe for compost?" I wondered. At least I could try to be ready for the next gardening season. I read:

> Lay the first layer of green matter directly on the earth so the worms can get into it. Alternate layers of vegetation and nitrogenous substances—dung, manure, and so on—add any organic material which will rot down easily—newspapers, wood shavings, egg shells, fish heads, kitchen garbage—and eventually cover the pile with a piece of old carpet or black plastic sheeting. Keep the heap watered under its covering. Let the decomposition heat to a temperature of at least 150 degrees Fahrenheit, killing the weed and disease spores—turn top to bottom, bottom to top with a garden fork, watering again, and eventually a nitrogen-loaded compost will be ready to enrich the garden, prevent weeds and keep the soil healthy.[1]

Strangely enough, this organic method of gardening reminds me of the ideal way to nurture children spiritually.

I believe the best spiritual growth comes when truth is applied to a child's everyday living, when the experiences and traumas and perplexities of common life are mixed with God's ideas, resulting in a nourishing fertilizer that enriches the soul.

Spiritual truth disassociated from everyday experience creates a disadvantageous growing environment, an inadequate spiritual ecology. The parent must become a master at grabbing the teachable, everyday moment. He or she must develop the ability to create compost, to pile on the stuff of everyday existence, and to mix it with spiritual truth.

Wes Willis, the vice-president of a major Sunday School curriculum house we've already quoted, has said:

> Instruction in the home has to be spontaneous—growing out of life. I am not opposed to specific times for teaching truth, but I think these should be a very small part of the religious training in the home. The family is a laboratory, and it's the ideal place to teach Christian truths in relationship, in tension, in context, as opposed to the school model where it's out of context, out of tension, and perhaps terribly distorted.[2]

Willis means that the emphasis on the spiritual training of children should be after the organic method. He means we must be about making rich, spiritual compost, rather than worrying about a family altar that exists only because someone got the idea that a family altar should exist.

I'm frequently asked at speaking engagements what method we used to spiritually train our children. When I reply that the Mains clan never has been very successful at a "family altar"—meaning a situation in which the patriarch gathers his spouse and offspring, preferably daily, and reads Scripture and prays—invariably a great sigh of relief goes up from the audience. Most in the crowd are having trouble establishing this traditional form, and they're feeling guilty about it.

Please understand, we have nothing against family altars. I know personally of families where it works remarkably well, and I give them credit. But I also know of families in which a family altar was forced on a disgruntled crew of children, with the result that their first lesson about spiritual things taught them such things were dull, boring, tedious, and to be avoided at all costs. And that's what I call a bad start for the spiritual training of a child.

Four Options for Building Family Spirituality

Every family determined to develop a spiritual environment will discover its own identity. But making the spiritual known in the Mains family has taken four specific forms which help us tremendously.

The first form is to honor Sunday with an understanding of the Sabbath principle.

The second is to hunt for and find God in our everyday world.

The third is to integrate moral and ethical content to the activity of decision making and living.

The last is to establish family health for the sake of each member advancing the Kingdom of God.

Every Christian family must determine how the spiritual is going to be "found" in its private life; and each parent must evaluate if the forms that are linked to spiritual activities are actually helping spiritual discovery or if they are hindering it.

If I had to choose between a formalized, structured, traditional family altar, and a family where the parents modeled lively, spiritual growth and where they knew how to make spiritual truth connect to daily life experience, I would always choose the latter. The best method by far of spiritual training is for the child to see spiritual life lived out. A family altar in a home where the parents have stagnated spiritually is deadly. It loudly says to the child: "We really don't believe in this stuff enough to make it work."

The ideal is for parents to grow spiritually themselves, to integrate spiritual truth with daily living, both good and bad. Following this comes formalized spiritual training.

Most of us have a tendency to reverse this order . . . and then we wonder why our children hate spiritual things, why they don't want to go to church, and why they leave the faith when they are adult enough (or courageous enough) to choose for themselves.

One reason for this abandonment is that we have made Christianity an ought-to, should-do, must-do kind of moralistic proposition based only on informational truth. One Christian educator says: "We need to be very, very careful that we don't see teaching historical fact as the sum total of teaching the Bible."[3]

We haven't clearly made the connections for our children between faith and unfair teachers, between faith and fights on the playgrounds, between faith and unkind friends. We pray in the most routine kind of way but don't really believe prayer has anything to do with a child's bad dreams, grades, fear of the dark, love of animals, or falling from a bicycle. We emphasize negative faith; our speech slants toward the negatives rather than toward the great, positive beauties of a life that follows Christ.

The parent must first experience, then reveal to his child how Christian faith weaves itself into the fabric of moment-by-moment, daily existence. A parent ought to be able to show a child his own growth journey, how sometimes he needs to be forgiven, how he struggles to reconcile relationships, how he seeks to expand his own mind as to who God is. The parent needs to show the child when faith works—when prayers are answered, when we are healed emotionally because of new theological understanding, when miracles occur, how well-being is a hallmark of the Christian life even in the midst of stress.

Again, Deuteronomy 6:6-7 is a cornerstone for any Christian educator seeking to develop a model for teaching a child about God. Here it is again:

> These commandments that I give you today are to be upon your hearts. Impress them on your children. Talk about them when you sit at home and when you walk along the road, when you lie down and when you get up.

"When you sit at home"—at mealtimes, times of conversation, times when guests are present, times when the children have come home from school. Compost ingredients!

"When you walk along the road"—as you journey, trips to the store, errands, vacations. More nitrogen-rich ingredients! You and your child are captive to each other. Turn off the ball game on the car radio. Be alert to all of those child questions such as, "Why did God make bad people?" Make up some questions of your own. Ask my husband's favorite: "How are you doing spiritually?"

"When you lie down"—at bedtime, that most rare moment when a child wants to keep his parent present, to review a day, to talk things over, to pray. Green matter, natural vegetation for sure!

This is the organic method.

This is creating a rich spiritual compost pile of daily experiences from which you can enrich your child's life of faith.

The organic method means the parent must be aware, must be alert, must use the tears, the disappointments, the spiritual pictures God has hidden in nature. It means he or she uses the pain of human relationships to show how spiritual truth fits with real life.

The parent who learns to cultivate his child's spiritual life organically, who learns to compost, will be demonstrating that Christianity fits, that it connects. You'll be showing that following Christ *works* in daily living.

Our youngest son, Jeremy, has a passionate interest in Japan. His interest began during a research project on the Samurai, expanded to taking private tutoring in the language, was nurtured by the interest of missionaries, extended to martial art lessons, and was encouraged by hours and hours of reading. David and I could only conclude that God had something to do with this special feeling and that he had some plan for Jeremy's future that included Japan. Consequently it was important to expose our son to the culture as soon as possible.

Upon Jeremy's strong insistence and after much prayer, for the summer of his fifteenth year we made arrangements through a third party for our son to travel alone to Japan, and to stay with a Japanese pastor in the city of Yonezawa. All the details had been worked out through written correspondence, and Jeremy was to be met in Tokyo by a Japanese woman who was a stranger to us all.

Our own schedule had been complicated that early summer. David and I had taken our once-in-a-lifetime real vacation to England, and I had left some of the travel arrangements for these trips to David's efficient secretary (who was in the process of moving out of state and training a replacement for her position).

We arrived home from overseas; within a couple of days the morning for Jeremy's departure was at hand. I drove him to O'Hare airport, parked the car, and we arrived at the United Airlines ticket counter about 8:00 A.M. His plane to Seattle, then on to Tokyo, was scheduled to depart at 10:00 A.M. A nice, orderly procedure with plenty of time to chat.

After the ticket had been processed, the woman at the counter checked Jeremy's passport. "And where is his visa for Japan?" she said.

The moment she asked the question I knew an essential detail had been overlooked. I had presumed, because nothing had been said to me, that Jeremy did not need a visa.

The details of our dilemma quickly presented themselves. It usually takes twenty-four hours to get a visa. The Japanese consulate was in downtown Chicago, and O'Hare was several miles and thousands of rush-hour vehicles away.

Another flight left for Japan the next day. But how would I make contact with the pastor in Japan? And what about the woman waiting for him in Tokyo? I didn't even think of the adjustment in fares due to change of schedule.

I decided to "go for it." As that decision was made I realized this was a teachable moment, unwelcome as it was. I said to Jeremy, "We have to believe that God is in all of life. He either wants to delay our getting on that airplane or he wants to teach us something very special through this experience. We are going to do the best we can and trust that God will help us in this dilemma."

(Jeremy informs me that although I did say this to him, my words didn't sound as calm as they read.)

I made arrangements with the woman at the counter to store Jeremy's luggage. While I was doing that, Jeremy got hold of his dad on the phone and the United worker found the address and phone number of the Japanese consulate. I grabbed the phone, asked David to pray and to call ahead to the Japanese consulate to explain our dilemma. Was there anything they could do to help us?

Jeremy and I ran to an elevated train of the Chicago Transit Authority, hopped aboard, and studied the map like crazy. I hoped I would choose the right stop.

On the ride into the city, I told Jeremy about a time I had been traveling through the refugee camps of the Far East. In Bangkok, my traveling companions and I were unable to procure visas to enter Bangladesh, even though the director of the organization had poured hundreds of thousands of dollars in relief and development projects into that country. He kept trying, getting more and more frustrated; but my attitude had been, "Maybe there's a reason."

The next morning, after our unsuccessful attempt, the newspapers reported that the very plane we had been scheduled to board had crashed on takeoff!

I was acutely aware that every attitude I struck in this frantic attempt was a modeling tool that Jeremy might have to use himself in a foreign country, far away from home, with minimal proficiency in the foreign tongue.

"Just keep praying," I whispered to him. "But pray, 'Lord, I believe you are in control. I believe you will help us. I believe you are going ahead.'"

"I know, Mom," he said. "What do you think I'm doing?"

I timed the trip to Chicago—forty minutes—and determined that if we did procure a visa, we would take a taxi back. Rush hour would be over by that time and we would be going out of the city. It would certainly be faster—and, miracle of miracles, I happened to have enough money after having gone to the bank the day before. If the consulate only opened at 9:00 A.M., if they would give us a visa, we just might make it.

We reached the consulate at 9:10; the visa office opened at 9:30. I spoke to the woman at the receptionist window. Yes, my husband had called, and I would be first in line. The door to the visa office opened at 9:25, and Jeremy and I stepped out onto Michigan Avenue in downtown Chicago fifteen minutes later with Japanese visa in hand. Twenty minutes to go until 10:00 A.M. O'Hare was all of thirty-five minutes away.

Jeremy began to falter. Time for some bucking up!

"Let's go for it, Jeremy! Sometimes planes are delayed, and maybe we can just make it."

In the taxi, Jeremy checked his ticket and discovered that the plane was not scheduled to leave until 10:10. Ten more precious minutes!

We wove through downtown traffic, hit the expressway, and reached the United ticket counter at exactly seven minutes past the hour. I walked to the first worker I could find; it was the same woman who had helped us earlier. She looked at me with surprise, but I didn't have to explain a thing. She called the gate, finished processing the ticket, turned to Jeremy and said, "Your baggage probably won't make it; but it will be sent to Tokyo on the next flight."

Jeremy and I hoofed it through the terminal to the appointed gate, where an attendant was waiting for our breathless arrival.

"Check in Tokyo for your luggage," I said with visions of my fifteen-year-old stranded in a foreign city, having missed his arrival contact, with no luggage to comfort him. "Sometimes they do miracles and get stuff on planes. It may be on the plane already."

We took a frantic last minute check: Had I handed him his passport? Did he have his ticket? He gave me a kiss. Then I admit I bragged a little: "Some kids have terrific moms, and some kids haven't got terrific moms. You got a terrific mom!"

But most of all, I thought, *don't ever forget what God has done for you here.*

I waited for the plane to take off, then called David and reported that by the grace of God, we had made it. And now, due to so much adrenaline pumping through my body, I was unfit for Illinois highways. I was going to have a cup of decaffeinated coffee, read the paper, and calm down. It might take an hour and a half.

The conclusion to this tale is that the appointed person met Jeremy in Tokyo, a woman who spoke little English. His bag did come through. She put him on a train after a transoceanic flight and he traveled alone two more hours to Yonezawa. The whole incredible journey left him completely unfazed. He was simply thrilled to be near a true love, Japan. Forget the other dramatics!

He had a wonderful summer, grew leaps and bounds, and didn't experience a moment of homesickness. But most of all, because of everything that had happened, he was utterly convinced that God was intimately involved in the stresses, the crises, and the schedules of our lives.

A good lesson to learn for children, teens, and adults alike!

One of the primary responsibilities God has given parents is *to seize the teachable moments.*

What's the recipe for a spiritual compost pile that will make your children grow? It's the stuff of daily ingredients mixed with a spiritually alert parent who is also growing spiritually, layered with Scripture that fits the experience, applied morning, noon, and night, all covered over with a carpet of prayer.

When such a mixture is shoveled on the family faith garden, it will fertilize, mulch, enrich, and heat the innermost self until it fully ripens before God.

I heartily suggest you try the organic method before it's too late.

NOTES

1. John Seymour, *The Self-Sufficient Gardner* (Garden City, N.J.: Doubleday-Dolphin, 1980), pp. 84-87.
2. Wes Willis, "How to Teach Your Child about God" series, "Chapel of the Air" radio program.
3. Ibid.

Couples' Discussion Questions

Early in our marriage we served with Youth for Christ, a national Christian youth organization. During those years we took a model for human development from Scripture which has continued to serve us well. Luke 2:52 reports, "And Jesus grew in wisdom and stature, and in favor with God and men."

When the Mains executive management team convenes—often in our board room, the local McDonald's restaurant—we evaluate ourselves and our children, drawing on the four simple measurements from this verse. Jesus grew in:

1. wisdom (mentally)
2. stature (physically)
3. in favor with God (spiritually)
4. in favor with men (socially)

Convene a meeting of your own executive board. Begin your personal evaluation session by choosing the family personality where there is the least conflict. Ask the following questions:

1. How is he/she doing mentally?
2. How is he/she doing physically?
3. How is he/she doing spiritually?
4. How is he/she doing socially?
5. How can each of us help this person or each other in the developmental process?

15 The Blessing

Karen

I overheard a mother say to her little child, "If you don't behave, God is going to punish you." Her words produced in me the same involuntary horror I feel every time car brakes squeal near the dangerous curve on Route 59, several hundred yards from our home. I wanted to say to that young woman, "There are many ways to teach a child about God, but believe me, this is not one of them!"

The parent who uses God as a whipping belt is teaching a child to fear God all right, but not in the scriptural way. Such ruinous approaches squelch faith development, shrivel ability to trust, and eventually lead the child to abandon not only this false idea of God, but Christianity itself.

My father worked at Moody Bible Institute for thirty-three years. He was a voice professor who eventually became the director of the music department. Three months after his retirement, he was stricken with mind-scrambling encephalitis. Four years later, after a slow and agonizing decline, he died.

I have a tape of his retirement luncheon which for years has sat in the back of my desk drawer. Countless times I've thought, *I would love to hear my father's voice. I should listen to that tape.* But I kept waiting for the time when I could afford the emotional disability I was sure the recording would prompt.

I listened to the tape today.

My father begins his farewell speech with words most appropriate to my theories about teaching children spiritual truth. He begins by talking about my grandfather:

> I had a wonderful father. He had a son that sometimes got into trouble. And, you know, you expect the switch; and instead of that, he blesses you, and the toughest discipline I think I've ever had were on occasions when, instead of the switch, my father blessed me.
>
> And how God works that way with us! We really are not worthy of these things; but somehow or another, in his great goodness, he blesses us.

I, too, had a wonderful father. I know he wasn't a perfect man. Sometimes the pressures of working with people all day, working with the fears and ego-needs of performers, took its toll. The struggle to make material ends meet tempted him to work harder than he should have. He often arrived home at 11:30 at night, after teaching private students in a downtown Chicago studio; and he invariably caught the 7:00 A.M. commuter train to the city. He gave voice lessons on Saturday in our home. He was the music minister of our church.

All this contributed to the stress of daily living. He wasn't a perfect man by any means, but he was a wonderful father.

When I think of my friends, the people I know very

well, I am often overwhelmed to realize that I am one of the few who received a father's blessing. There were times when I, too, deserved the switch. I'd misbehaved in attitude or in deed, but my father would take me into his arms, say the words (and I heard them so often), "What seems to be the problem?" I would tell him out of my anger or frustration or tears. He would listen, respond sympathetically, and invariably send me away with some kind of positive prophecy. He would say, "Now, sweet. This seems bad to you at this moment. But I know you. I believe in you. I believe you have the capacity to handle this difficulty. Perhaps you've made a mistake, but I know you can make it right."

Off I would go with his love and his blessing. And I would invariably turn myself toward healthy behavior. I would choose to rectify my mistakes and do what was right. I would apologize to the wronged party. I would seek maturity and accept responsibility for my own error—all because I had a father who expected that I, his well-loved daughter, had the capacity and desire to live a righteous and moral life.

My father knew that punitive discipline—blows and retribution—was not nearly as effective as the discipline of blessing. I can't ever remember him sending me to my room, establishing a curfew, docking my allowance. My father understood that most of the time I would choose to behave rather than to shake his good faith in me or to lose his blessing.

What is a blessing?

Gary Smalley and John Trent have written a book with the very title *The Blessing*. In it they examine the Old Testament patriarchal blessings such as the one Abraham gave to Isaac and Isaac gave to Jacob and Jacob gave to his sons.

Genesis 48-49 records the emotional moment when

the sons of Israel gathered by their father's deathbed. Israel blesses Joseph's sons:

> So Joseph brought his sons close to him, and his father kissed them and embraced them. . . . Israel reached out his right hand and put it on Ephraim's head, though he was the younger, and crossing his arms, he put his left hand on Manasseh's head. . . . Then he blessed Joseph and said,
>
> May the God before whom my fathers
> Abraham and Isaac walked,
> the God who has been my shepherd
> all my life to this day,
> the Angel who has delivered me from all harm
> —may he bless these boys.
> May they be called by my name
> and the names of my fathers
> Abraham and Isaac,
> and may they increase greatly
> upon the earth (Genesis 48:10-16).

The authors closely examine the scriptural examples and conclude that there are five ingredients common to patriarchal blessings. There is

1. meaningful touch;
2. a spoken word;
3. expression of high value;
4. picturing a special future, and;
5. an active commitment on the part of the blesser.

Building their book around the premise that every child needs to receive his parents' blessing, the authors conclude that one of the great faith cripplers in children happens when parents withhold this blessing. Parents injure their children when they don't touch meaningfully, when they don't speak the words which communicate high value in the child or which picture a special future, when they don't communicate an active commitment to help the child achieve that future.

After reading *The Blessing* and after hearing my father's recorded words today, I realize I received my father's blessing, if not daily, then at least every week of my life. I'm convinced it is one of the reasons I have so eagerly embraced God on the most personal levels of my life. Parents who want to teach their children about God must learn to impart this kind of holy blessing themselves.

This means we must understand that when we touch meaningfully, when we pat or caress, when we embrace, when we give back rubs, when we wipe away the tears or push back the hair, we can impart God's touch to the child. Scripture tells us how Christ "blessed the children." Mark 10:13 says, "People were bringing little children to Jesus to have him touch them, but the disciples rebuked them. When Jesus saw this, he was indignant. . . . and he took the children in his arms, put his hands on them and blessed them."

When we say to a child, "I know you can do it," or, "I thank God that of all the boys in the world, he gave you to me as my son," or, "I'm so proud of how you handled that difficult situation," we are giving verbal blessings by expressing high value. When we project a future for the child, when we realistically help them to assess their goals, we are giving a blessing.

One of our adult children was telling me how she tried to explain our form of discipline to one of her friends. "You never punished us," she said. "You sat down and talked things over. When I told Jennifer that you disciplined us by communication, she said, 'Oh no, I'd rather be punished!'"

Even verbal discipline can take the form of a blessing.

If a child hasn't done his job, we can say, "I chose this task for you because I believe you are old enough and skilled enough to do it well. It disappoints me that you haven't done this job; but I still think you are capable of doing the task. Doing this job is one of the ways you can please me; it is one of the ways you can develop your capabilities."

How different this "come-now-let-us-reason-together" approach is from that of the parent who casts curses: "I knew you couldn't do it! You never do anything right that I tell you to do. You're never going to amount to anything! You'll be a bum for sure."

When that kind of talk hits the air, traffic is screeching on Route 59 again. Collision ahead! It's not a parental blessing. It's not the way the God who believes in us works. But it is the tactic of the great accuser of our souls, Satan.

Are we giving blessings or curses to our children?

If blessing is not a part of our lexicon, we may be making it difficult for our children ever to experience God's blessing. We may actually be teaching them that God is a punitive God, lurking in the heavenly bushes just to catch them when they fall, waiting to punish them with a big and nasty stick.

(And just in case some of us didn't know, God is not like that. He isn't!)

Though God disciplines us, I believe most often he does it like my father, through undeserved blessing. Over and over he gives us what we haven't earned: life itself, the availability of his constant love, redemption through the sacrifice of his Son, the empowering of his Spirit, an eternal inheritance.

If you are giving blessing to your children, don't ever stop.

If you are not, perhaps the place you need to begin today is with Esau's plea, but directed toward our great Heavenly Father: "Bless me, even me, Oh my God!" so that out of the blessing you receive from him you can bless the child he has placed in your hand.

Couples' Discussion Questions

Take some quiet, uninterrupted time to ask yourself these questions regarding the blessing:

1. Does my touch bless my child like Christ's touch blessed the children? Or do my children cringe from the touch of my hand? Do they flinch? Stiffen their bodies?
2. Am I speaking verbal blessings? Or am I speaking verbal curses? If I would put my words to my children or about my children in a balance, which side would fall with most weight, the negative side or the positive?
3. Do I really believe that my child has the potential to amount to something? Or am I secretly afraid he or she will turn out bad?
4. Did I ever really have my parents' blessing? When did that happen, and how frequently?

16 Humble Parents Make Good Parents

Karen

I have a godly friend who applies spiritual understanding to her work as a therapist. Recently she said something about healthy parenting that intrigued me: "You know, many Christian parents concern me. They do the very same things that non-Christian parents do. They take a completely secular approach to child-rearing. They're often rigidly authoritarian, they use anger to manipulate, they load on the guilt—but they have the audacity to call it 'Christian.' It isn't really Christian at all; it isn't Christlike. They're simply adapting old, harmful patterns of parenting and using Christianity as an excuse."

I agree. Many Christian parents act as though their main role in life is to negate their children. And that is decidedly un-Christlike.

James Fowler, a Harvard-trained theologian with a background in developmental psychology, wrote a book titled, *Stages of Faith*. It's the result of ten years of research on the developmental path that faith takes in human beings. Fowler warns that one of the most common mistakes parents make is excessive negative moralism.

> Usually this is done with the best of intentions. It is a combination of wanting to nurture our children in the faith but not having a great deal of confidence in our ability.[1]

Children interpret this kind of spiritual training to mean that their parents expect them to be bad. Fowler says that allowing children to hear and see the dailiness of their parents' faith is much more potent than sitting down and saying, "We're going to get this straight, once and for all."

Robert Burgess, while doing research on neglectful families, found that members of such families interact with each other much less than do members of healthier, control families. When they did interact—when they spoke to one another, spent time with each other—the contacts tended to be negative.

These neglectful mothers and fathers gave positive input to their children at a rate approximately 50 percent lower than did the control families; neglectful mothers displayed rates of negative behavior more than twice as high as the control mothers, with fathers being 75 percent higher.[2]

I suspect there are many Christian parents who would be shocked to discover that their teaching and modeling of the moral dimensions of Christianity fall woefully close to the negative profile of the neglectful parents in Burgess's studies.

To these parents, a child is not really a person of value. His or her ideas are not important. The child is not listened to or really heard. He's seen only as an extension of the parent's personality.

The parent thinks of the child as bad, or a nuisance, or a pest, or a mess-maker, or as trouble. A clue to this kind of parent is the tone of voice used when addressing the child or when talking about the child. It's filled with nuances of anger, sarcasm, impatience, frustration, intolerance, exasperation; it's without warmth, pride, tenderness, delight.

This kind of parenting does incalculable damage. It models a bad example of relationships for the child on the purely human level, and worst of all, it creates a hostile atmosphere in which to teach spiritual truth.

I like the title of one of Anne Ortland's books: *Children Are Wet Cement*. We all need to ask, "What impressions am I making on my child?" We must remember that our child will carry those impressions, those internal markings, for the rest of his or her life.

Donald Joy in *Moral Development Foundations* points out that adult faith sees life as dynamic. Like a tree, where growth is measured by the rings in the trunk, each part of the life of the organism remains part of the matured entity. The seedling is present even though the tree stands fifty years tall; the past child is part of the present adult.

We parents must keep this dynamic in mind. What we give to our children now is the organic matter out of which their adult self will mature. The seedling is part of the whole; it is not discarded like the skin of a snake, left to mold in the sun on a rock. That self, cherished or disaffirmed, is part of the present adult.

Now, all of us have a tendency to negate our children at some point. We get tired of messes and noise and childish inconsideration. We weary of the endless responsibility. No one warned us at birth that we would someday become a parent forever after . . . and not necessarily happily.

I can remember one young man who boldly exhorted me about my negative attitude toward one of my children. At the time, I would have liked to pour a bucket of cold water on his presumptuous head (he was childless at the time). I learned instead that not only was he right in correcting me, but he was the voice of God speaking a warning to me in human form. I became utterly grateful for his timely intervention.

The point of parenting which we must all remember is that adults demonstrate to their children the right way to behave. The point of Christian parenting is that we must show what it means to be like Christ; in fact, we point to Jesus by treating our children the same way he would treat them. We show the child what it means to live a Christian life by living a Christian life.

This does not mean we have to be perfect. What a wonderful freedom to jettison that ancient relic of misparenting lore! We can trash the old, authoritarian insistence: "I can do no wrong. I am the parent; you are the child. I know more than you do. I am perfect."

We do not have to be perfect, and it is far, far better to demonstrate to our children how to behave as Christians when we fall short. They will be imperfect, they will live in an imperfect world. They will struggle with imperfect relationships, fulfill imperfect destinies. What tools we give them to survive, to overcome, to conquer, when we have the courage to demonstrate our own humanity!

This works out very practically. What happens when there's a breach in the family, when a relationship needs to be mended? If our children see our pain, if they see our struggle to renew what has been broken and our attempts to assess where we have contributed to the breakdown, if they hear or even join in on our prayers and watch as we confess our errors and witness our attempts at reconciliation, then they will experience our joy when restoration comes. And one day they'll try the same thing for their own bruised relationships.

That is healthy modeling of the Christian life. One Christian educator has said, "It's much less important for parents to be right than it is for parents to show how to act when they are wrong. If I lose my temper and get mad at my son, I need to apologize to him and show him how to deal with getting mad inappropriately. I've sinned. I've received forgiveness from God. Now I say to him, 'Would you forgive me?' "[3]

That's easy to say. But how do we overcome our tendency to ape the secular, unredeemed society around us?

I've concluded that humility is the very best attitude for curing this tendency. Howard Hendricks has said, "God gives us children to teach us about ourselves."

It's much more profitable for the Christian parent to realize that his child may have as much to teach him about the spiritual life as he has to teach his child. My children give me clues as to what Christ meant when he said, "Unless you become as a little child, you cannot enter the kingdom of heaven." They have a natural faith which often shames my own faltering belief- system, buffeted as it often is by a too-active adult rationality.

Humility is the greatest gift I can bring to parenting my children.

I am humbled when I realize that I am only an earthly surrogate for their true Heavenly Parent, God. I am humbled when I acknowledge that these children are not here to make me look good, but to make God look good.

I'm humbled when I realize that my role as a parent is not to rear these children in my own image, but to raise them in the image of the One who loves them more than I can ever love them. It's hard to get proud when I consider him who is infinitely more concerned about their well-being than I ever will be, who has a plan and a future for them I don't even understand.

I'm humbled when I realize that though I'm a surrogate parent at one level of my relationship with my children, at another level they are my brothers and sisters because of our common unity in Christ. In this we are equals.

I'm humbled when I realize there is much that I cannot show them, tell them, demonstrate to them, teach them. I am at best an inadequate human. My role is to step aside, bend my knee in faithful prayer, and allow the Holy Spirit to do in their lives what I will never be able to do.

I'm humbled when I realize I must be very careful in my persuasions, in my petty and private prejudices, and through my own inadequate growth I must be careful not to get in the way of God's ideas, plans, and design for their place in this world.

Yes, humility is the best attitude we can bring to our task of teaching our children about God.

When analyzing our parenting skills, many of us realize we have a long way to go to develop the abilities necessary to create a home environment conducive to effective spiritual training. But take heart; these skills can be learned. David and I are learning them all the time.

These days, I'm learning how to be a parent to adult children. I'm learning how to be a mother-in-law, how to truly welcome my offspring when they return home, how to reorder my near-empty nest. We can all learn how to be good parents. The skills are learnable.

In fact, one of the most instructive manuals on parenting is a book with which I hope you're intimately familiar. That book is called the Holy Scripture. What we often don't understand (but which should give us great hope) is that we can apply all the relational teachings from this book to the way we treat our children. Most of us have a tendency to focus only on a few verses, such as this one from Ephesians: "Fathers, do not exasperate your children. . . ."

But how about all those other relational verses such as: "Love must be sincere. . . . rejoice with those who rejoice; mourn with those who mourn. . . . Live in harmony with one another. Do not be proud. . . . Do not repay anyone evil for evil . . . live at peace with everyone. . . ."?

This is just a sampling of verses applicable to the parent/child relationship, and they are all from one chapter, Romans 12. Think of the rich, biblical resources we could plumb if we thought of the Scriptures as a handbook on parenting! In fact, let's do just that in the work session that follows.

NOTES

1. James Fowler, *Stages of Faith* (San Francisco: Harper & Row, 1981).
2. Robert Burgess, "How to Teach Your Child about God" series, "Chapel of the Air" radio program.
3. Ibid.

Couples' Discussion Questions

Take one section of the New Testament. Romans 12 would be a good start. Consider it a manual on child-rearing, a parent's handbook on how to act like Christ. View it with new eyes, then ask hard questions like:

1. Do we treat our child like this? Like this?
2. Would Christ treat our child the way we are treating him or her?
3. Does Christ treat us the way we are treating our child, or are we imposing an old, secular, non-Christian system of parenting on our child?
4. Do we really think our child has something to teach us? Or do we think we know everything?
5. How do these Scriptures suggest that we change our parenting procedures?

I guarantee that this exercise will be a learning experience. And if it is, be glad! You are beginning to really be able to teach your child about God.

17 Father's Feet in Mother's Shoes

David

Karen often says, "God opens doors for me, and David pushes me through!"

I don't like to think of it that way, but I do know we all need a little encouragement now and then. So when the invitation came for her to travel for six to seven weeks through the refugee camps of the world to write something fresh about these human dilemmas, I thought it was an opportunity she couldn't miss. Without being fully aware of what I was committing myself to, I volunteered to be housefather for our four children—all of whom were still at home, two of whom were still in grade school.

The lessons those weeks taught me about servant leadership were frustrating, fascinating, and lasting. I also learned what it meant to be a wife and mom. A broadcast I wrote toward the end of Karen's journey well describes my learning process—it was an experience all men should have. The broadcast sounded like this:

Karen has been gone about six weeks now, but it seems much longer. When she returns in a few days from her trip—an extended visit to refugee centers in Asia, the Middle East, and Africa—I know she will have a great many experiences to share with the family. And I have a few of my own to recount to her!

This is the longest period of time that our four children—Randy, 17; Melissa, 15; Joel, 11; and Jeremy, 8—have experienced with Daddy at the helm of the home. I want to record my observations for posterity before they are totally overshadowed by Karen's graphic reports.

I've grouped my observations into five neat personal reactions to this unusual role as househusband.

1. Hey! Didn't I Just Do That Yesterday?

This special reaction didn't occur immediately. In fact, during the first couple of weeks, I really enjoyed doing dishes, picking things up, observing how nice the living room looked right after I vacuumed. Even making the bed was rather fun. Not that I had never done any of these tasks before—it's just that I hadn't seen them as *my* daily responsibility. I did now.

It must have been about a month into my pilgrimage that this new thought came to me: *It seems like what needs to be done today is a lot like what needed to be done yesterday.* How many times do I have to make this bed? Where did all these dirty clothes come from? Who messed up the couch again? Can't Joel think to practice his clarinet without having to be reminded?

When I got home from the office on Wednesday it seemed just about like it did Tuesday, which was basically a replay of Monday. Somewhere in my memory I vaguely recall Karen speaking of how women have to do the same jobs over and over, and my answer was, "Uh-huh."

2. Who Made Me Judge over You?

That's what Jesus said in Luke 12 when two brothers wanted him to settle a dispute regarding an inheritance. I guess I had never realized the number of petty squabbles that can take place between siblings. "But I had it first, Daddy!" "He took an extra turn!" "Shouldn't he have to pick it up? He got it out!"

This second discovery called for great wisdom and patience. I walked my two little guys through their difficulties and tried to show them how to resolve such issues on their own. It didn't take long before I realized they weren't incorporating what I was teaching them. My reasonable approach to the joy of submitting didn't fit most of their problems anyway.

What does Karen do?" I wondered. *There has to be some secret she has, because obviously this role of wisely determining who is innocent and who is guilty is pretty demanding.*

3. Who Is the Mystery Messer?

Before leaving for the office in the morning, the house was usually in decent shape. But when I returned about 5:15 p.m., somehow the peanut butter jar was always out, dishes cluttered the sink, books were on the floor, mail was scattered here and there, light bulbs were burning, and the dining room table resembled the Indianapolis Speedway—except the cars were of the matchbox variety.

Yes, there was something strange about this daily phenomenon: Nobody claimed responsibility for it. So innocent were the faces of my children, I got the feeling that were I to leave the office and arrive home fifteen minutes before anyone returned from school, I would still find a sweater by the back door, a milk carton on the counter, various items strewn on the stairs, and a few volumes of the encyclopedia missing.

For a while, I suspected that our West Highland terrier was the secret phantom. I knew that Melissa's cat, Masie, was too dumb and too lazy to accomplish that much clutter day after day. Maybe a house-wrecking demon visited while I was at work? A mystery messer!

4. How Come No One's Clapping?

This one has been the hardest of all for me to swallow. As an executive, I'm used to affirmation, expressions of thanks, and a certain amount of respect. During the past weeks with Karen away, I presumed this would rub off in the house also—especially when I went out of my way to make certain that things were "just like when Mom was around."

Guess what? Silence.

Oh, not total silence, but I haven't received a standing ovation, either. I've come to realize that housework is just not the kind of thing that evokes a great deal of praise. But miss a cue, and people notice! "How come I don't have any clean socks?" "Hey, Dad, we're out of milk!" "Guess what? You forgot to come home early to drive me to baseball practice!"

Running a *smooth* house is just expected; it's not something anyone raves about.

5. Whatever Happened to Peace and Quiet?

Never before have I so greatly appreciated the luxury of a private office, a secretary to take my calls, and a staff which protects my study time.

Funny, but until this past month I had never really thought of home as a noisy place. But to listen attentively to most of what the four kids say, to monitor needs, to care for Jeremy who came down with the chicken pox the day after Karen had flown off to Hong Kong and only 7-Up sounded good and I bought him a big bottle and put it in the refrigerator and someone else drank it— and "don't cry, I'll get you another one"—is just plain work.

"Didn't I tell you to clean your room, Melissa?"

"I'm sorry, but Daddy can't be bothered right now. Can't you see I'm trying to pray? It will just have to wait."

"How come nobody told me there was a letter from your mother in the mail this morning? What do you mean, I was praying and said 'Don't bother me right now'? "

"How many weeks have these library books been overdue?"

"*Who* wants to have dinner with us?—Please turn down that record player!—and does anybody know where the thermometer is?"

"Who made that wisecrack about home-sweet-home?"

And aside to myself: "Never was there a more inappropriate place to try practicing saintliness."

Actually, I thought I had the peace and quiet problem worked out. I'd just wait until everyone was in bed, and then the cherished calm I desired would be mine. This tactic worked great for a couple of weeks; then, alas, it seemed that when everyone else was finally asleep, so was my mind! At least, it had a difficult time tracking what Isaiah was saying (I didn't master the prophet like I'd hoped).

Well, I've learned a lot these last weeks about myself, and about God, too. Now I see him more as a complete parent, and not just from my male viewpoint. Talking with him, I've had some new things to say. Things like:

> Father, thanks for being willing to do for me today a lot of the same things you did yesterday—and the day before.
>
> Thanks for attempting to teach me to pray, "Forgive us our trespasses, as we forgive those who trespass against us." That has helped me to solve a whole lot of interpersonal problems without whimpering to you for arbitration.
>
> And Lord, this "mystery messer syndrome" must aggravate heaven. For my own sake, please don't let me get by with causing problems by

messing things up when you've worked hard at putting things in order. Thank you for the many ways you make life enjoyable—for providing for our needs, giving us each day our daily bread. I clap my hands regarding your steady performance. You care for me exceptionally well. You really do!

And Lord, how do you handle the infinite demands that come your way daily? How do you function with no rest—never having time for yourself? Don't answer: I know you are not to be compared with my limitations! But please know this—that in these past weeks you have expanded my tiny mind to comprehend you in a new way, and I am glad. *Amen.*

I fear that after this my kids are going to demand equal time, so let me sum up by saying that praise is due our Lord for his complete parenting. Though we call him Father, I've come to believe he also does some outstanding mothering.

I'm not the first David to explore such a thought. In Psalm 103, King David writes tenderly regarding his Lord,

> Bless the LORD, O my soul; and all that is within me,
> bless His holy name!
> Bless the LORD, O my soul, and forget not all His benefits. . . .
> Who heals all your diseases. . . .
> Who crowns you with lovingkindness and tender mercies,
> Who satisfies your mouth with good things. . . .
> The LORD is merciful and gracious, slow to anger and abounding in mercy.

> He will not always strive with us, nor will He keep His anger forever.
>
> The LORD pities those who fear Him, for He knows our frame, He remembers that we are dust.
>
> The mercy of the LORD is from everlasting to everlasting on those who fear Him,
>
> and His righteousness to children's children (NKJV).

I have, of course, been selecting certain lines from this Psalm, but that doesn't change the point. The conclusion of Psalm 103 echoes the very thing I have been saying about learning new lessons while my wife is away traveling around the world:

> Bless the LORD in all places of His dominion,
>
> Bless the LORD, O my soul!

18 Why Doesn't Anyone Tell Me I'm Doing a Good Job?

David and Karen

A young mother of two sighed and said, "I just wish someone would tell you when you're doing a good job."

We know what she means. Plenty of experts have studied what is *wrong* with the family. Teachers will make appointments when your child has a behavior problem. Grandparents know when you're not doing it "the way they used to do it." Youth leaders and Sunday School teachers, neighbors and friends, sociologists and Christian educators all have plenty of evaluations as to what is going wrong with spouses, parents, and their offspring.

Even self-evaluation is tenuous; the definitive results of parenting are long-range. Moms and dads often can't determine success or failure until their children are adults and parents themselves!

That's why we were so relieved to find some excellent studies which reveal the ingredients of family well-being. Finally, we had some measurements other than our own intuitions by which to gauge what we were doing.

Dr. Nick Stinnett, while professor and chairman of the Department of Human Development and the Family at the University of Nebraska, launched a research project aimed at examining the common characteristics of well-being in some three thousand families. Many of the couples included rated themselves highly in terms of marriage happiness and satisfaction in parent-child relationships.

Researchers found they could divide the characteristics of healthy families into six main categories. Strong families:

1. were committed to the family;
2. spent time together;
3. had good family communication;
4. expressed appreciation to each other;
5. were able to solve problems in a crisis;
6. *and had a spiritual commitment*.

If we were to hold a casual brainstorming session trying to define the common characteristics of family health, we might name all or most of these points. But it is extraordinarily affirming when expensive and time-consuming scientific research substantiates our intuition.

Point number six is important to our discussion of spirituality in the family. Stinnett and his team found that healthy families are highly religious. Now, this religious involvement may not be Christian, and it may not be aligned with an organized church, but these healthy families considered themselves to be highly committed to their spiritual lives.

The chief characteristic of these families' religious expression was a *faith system which affected and was integrated practically into personal, day-to-day living*. These families were not content with a formalized, intellectualized, theoretical, academic faith. Stinnett makes a connection between his team's discoveries about the religious expression of healthy families and sociological research which also indicates an association between family and marriage success and an active religious association.[1]

We were so impressed with Stinnett's research that we decided to use it in our own family. Using the six common characteristics of healthy families as an outline, we first evaluated ourselves, then asked our children to do the same.

Because all the studies on well-being maintain that a healthy environment in families is determined by an unusually strong relationship between husband and wife, we first asked ourselves how we as parents were doing. Then we asked the children: How did they rate our family life? Where were we good? Where did we need to improve?

We discovered that our offspring viewed some areas in a different light than we did! These differing viewpoints made possible excellent discussions, with the result that we began to work harder on certain aspects of family well-being we might otherwise have ignored.

These characteristics were so valuable to us personally that we began to teach them on the radio, in conferences, and in seminar ministries. To the characteristics of family healthiness developed by researcher Stinnett and his colleagues, we added some of the research definitions discovered through the work of Dolores Curran. Curran distinguished fifteen characteristics of family health after polling some five hundred professionals who deal with family life. Our expanded outline, combining both of these excellent sources, looks like this:

1. *Healthy families have good communication.*

The healthy family listens and responds rather than listening and reacting. In many family discussions, parents and children don't really hear. Defense mechanisms go up, people think only about how they are going to reply. There is no real learning from each other, no real empathy

Is Belief Important?

Dolores Curran, syndicated columnist specializing in the family, queried professional family workers—teachers, doctors, pastors, Boy and Girl Scout leaders, social workers—and asked them to list qualities of healthy family life. Some 551 respondents defined fifteen common categories, one of which was "the healthy family has a shared religious core."

Curran amplifies this characteristic in her excellent and helpful book, *Traits of a Healthy Family*. She says:

1. Faith in God plays a foundational role in family life;
2. A religious core strengthens the family support system;
3. Parents feel a strong responsibility for passing on the faith in positive and meaningful ways.

"Passing on the faith is not an easy job today," she writes, "but parents in healthier families are not abandoning the attempt. They recognize the foolishness of relying solely on such old reliables as Sunday School, Bible verses, and confirmation to furnish lifelong religious belief. . . . Perhaps one father summed it up best for those striving to share a strong religious core within their family, 'Without it, nothing else makes much sense—all the work and the worry— what's the point if you don't believe in anything?'"[1] And with those words, we, the Mainses, do most heartily agree!

1. Dolores Curran, *Traits of a Healthy Family* (Minneapolis: Winston Press, 1983) pp. 247-261.

with the feelings and desires of one another.

Good communication includes patterns for reconciliation. Well-being in the family demands that parents and children find ways to deal with problems, learn the meaning of forgiveness, develop an instinct for when and where not to approach one another, know when to end fruitless, heated discussions. Two prayers for the marriage ceremony from *The Book of Common Prayer* give a picture of tools for the work of reconciliation:

> Give them grace, when they hurt each other, to recognize and acknowledge their fault, and to seek each other's forgiveness and yours. *Amen.*
>
> Make their life together a sign of Christ's love to this sinful and broken world, that unity may overcome estrangement, forgiveness heal guilt, and joy conquer despair. *Amen.*

Healthy families have good communication by controlling television viewing; by recognizing non-verbal messages and learning to correctly interpret these signals; by refusing to use harmful turn-off words and insulting put-down phrases; by eliminating negative labels, insults, and name-calling.

One of the characteristics of good communication in these families is the importance placed on intensity and spontaneity in conversation. There is a liveliness in group discussions. These folks laugh, they are intensely serious . . . and they interrupt one another! What is important is the communication of ideas and feelings, not merely the propriety of verbal exchange.

Part of good communication is the ability to encourage independent thought and emotion. These families place little priority on what is known as "group-think." Individuality and uniqueness is valued.

Communication: Key to a Healthy Marriage

Since good communication is so central to health, we have included this self-evaluation tool to help you assess your own abilities in this area. Evaluate your own self (not your spouse), but do make sure you discuss the results.

Circle the number that best indicates where you fall on the scale, and enter the total in the space at the bottom.

I am constantly aware of the importance of communication in the family.	10 9 8 7 6 5 4 3 2 1	I need to be reminded over and over about the importance of communication in the family.
I understand fully the significance of non-verbal communication. I listen to what my family members' bodies say.	10 9 8 7 6 5 4 3 2 1	I constantly need to be reminded that there is such a thing as non-verbal communication.
I have learned how to keep my family's attention when I talk.	10 9 8 7 6 5 4 3 2 1	The moment I start to talk I sense I have lost the interest of everyone.
Rate me a 10 as a listener.	10 9 8 7 6 5 4 3 2 1	Give me a 1. I'm a terrible listener.
I work to adjust my conversation to the vocabulary and interest levels of others.	10 9 8 7 6 5 4 3 2 1	I know I'm often too technical, over my family's heads.
I make a point to affirm my family.	10 9 8 7 6 5 4 3 2 1	I have a tendency to think my family knows of my pride in them without speaking of it.

I work hard to ask questions that show I am interested in their worlds.	10 9 8 7 6 5 4 3 2 1	I'm afraid I've slipped into a habit of telling rather than of wanting to know about them.
I am not afraid to initiate discussions in areas where there will be disagreement.	10 9 8 7 6 5 4 3 2 1	I avoid confrontation and if the issues are forced, I become defensive.
I love to participate in the give-and-take of free-wheeling conversational exchange and I encourage this in the family.	10 9 8 7 6 5 4 3 2 1	I feel uptight when when there are too many ideas, challenges, and verbal fireworks.
I work to make my communications clear and concise and I seem to be well-received.	10 9 8 7 6 5 4 3 2 1	There seems to be confusion when I ommunicate. I often feel misunderstood.

TOTAL _____

If you rated yourself 80 or above, you appear to possess outstanding family communication skills. If you rated yourself between 60 and 80, you may be getting a signal that some improvement is necessary if you are to reach your family communication potential. If you rated yourself below 60, some substantial improvement is indicated.

2. *Healthy families spend time together.*

This is the area where our children felt we needed to improve. During intense discussion, all four of our offspring insisted that Dad worked too hard (labeling him a workaholic), and explained that while we were great at planned occasions— putting dates for special family times into the calendar and honoring these—we were "terrible" at the spontaneous, grab-the- moment, put-your-feet-up-on-the-table-and-let-your-hair-down, unplanned moments. There was always something more important to do.

We heard their complaints, reluctantly came to agreement, and began work to change deeply entrenched habits. As parents, we had rated ourselves pretty highly in the area of spending time together (thinking of the yearly Stratsford, Ontario Shakespeare Festival, the monthly Lord's Day Eve meals, etc.), but we realized our children had a need for another style of expression in this area.

Author Curran points to some specifics of good family time-planning:

- activities are prioritized
- mealtime conversation is valued; the dinner meal becomes an important gathering for the exchange of daily happenings. TV is turned off.
- work and outside activities are not allowed to infringe routinely on family time.

3. *Healthy families encourage and affirm one another.*

Members of healthy families deliberately note whatever good traits they see in one another; they do not leave their observations unstated. Healthy families work at speaking encouragement. They understand that support does not mean pressure: "If I say these wonderful things, you will have to live up to them." They maintain a basically positive mood, even in the face of negative circumstances. They know that genuine approval and support helps children develop healthy self-esteem, and they aren't worried that words of affirmation will cause conceit.

4. *Healthy families have a commitment to the family.*

Husband and wife share important values. These families treasure their legends and characters, reiterating the past for members of the younger generation. Elders are honored and babies are welcomed. They make a deliberate effort to gather as a people, and they cherish family traditions and rituals which are viewed as a means of enriching the rigorous nature of life. They celebrate that life in all its dimensions as they celebrate one another.

5. *Healthy families have a religious orientation.*

Much has been said about this characteristic already; more will be said in the epilogue.

6. *Healthy families deal positively with a crisis.*

Curran points out that part of family well-being is the expectation that problems and crises are integral to daily living. Difficulties will come and they will have to be faced. Healthy families develop skills which recognize those potentially serious problems and deal with them early. Such families refuse to catastrophize minor circumstances, they allow for negotiation in crisis, and find ways to help one's own family group. They are unafraid to seek aid from professionals when a difficulty is too big to handle alone. Healthy families stay together in bad times as well as good times.

Negative circumstances can show our weaknesses or highlight our strengths, and having lived through years of family life where we dealt with several crises, minor and major, we feel it would be of benefit to find measurements that help us "know when we are doing a good job" by focusing on this characteristic a bit more.

We met Dr. Bill Wilson in Washington, D.C., during a gathering of conservative Christians hoping to influence federal legislation on family issues. Sitting over breakfast at McDonald's, Dr. Wilson told us the story of his conversion while leading a Boy Scout camping trip into the wilds. He testified to an experience of God's love so intense he knew he had been converted: "But I didn't know to what!" The experience was so life-changing that, while telling his story nearly twenty years later, tears still flowed down his cheeks.

Wilson eventually returned to his research and psychiatric work on the teaching staff of Duke University. He began to examine the implications of religious belief and spiritual practice on both physical and psychological health. He instituted a course which examined the tenets of Christianity in relation to psychiatry and eventually gathered some sixty residents in psychiatry who began to integrate their faith with their work.

Much of the resulting research data of these efforts gives a scientific basis for spiritual life in the Christian family. Research work is even now being conducted, and one of the greatest needs in the academic and scientific community is for individuals to see the importance of factoring in the spiritual as part of their investigations.

Wilson shows that crisis is indeed an important determinant of family healthiness. "How do we handle the ordinary occurrences of everyday crisis, and what strengths are we developing to cope with those catastrophes which are not ordinary, but which can strike any family?" are two helpful questions to consider *before* the extraordinary occurs.

Wilson reports that crises often develop because of family inadequacies in several areas:

1. inadequate interpersonal relationships;
2. cultural diversity;
3. conflicting roles;
4. economic and`other pressures;
5. societal class membership pressures, and;
6. unrealized aspirations.[2]

According to Wilson, characteristics of happy and harmonious families which produce children of worth include:

1. the husband and wife love each other (the most critical factor);
2. there is order in the home;

3. roles of husband and wife are well delineated, complementary, and traditional;
4. discipline is just but not harsh;
5. parents subscribe to traditional values, live by them, and teach them to their children, and;
6. parents have a philosophy to live by which makes a favorable difference in their lives and which incorporates their value system.[3]

Interestingly, and despite the popular claims prophesying the demise of the traditional family, these six characteristics have their roots in a basic Judeo-Christian heritage. While modern philosophies have sought to deemphasize the spiritual and traditional, scorning these values and trying to change them, investigations arising out of their very challenge have actually authenticated the importance of a biblically-ordered family structure.

Various studies focusing on some of the more urgent societal problems—juvenile delinquency, alcoholism, heroin addiction and chaotic personalities—have now demonstrated that one of the primary reasons these deviancies develop is a family structure that departs from the traditional scheme above. Research is continually validating the wisdom of traditional family structure. One project examined good emotional health in young males and strongly related their well-being to these principles.[4]

Wilson emphasizes that the husband/wife relationship centers in the lives of two people who have learned to live and work together *complementarily*. They have developed a good subsystem of leadership; they respect and model respect for one another's viewpoints. Generational boundaries are well-defined—the child doesn't act like a parent, the parent doesn't act like the child— and there are no competing family member cliques.

Although their approaches to discipline, listening

styles, avocational and vocational interests may be different, the parents are nevertheless united on core questions of the meaning of life and long-range goals, and they reach consensus on child- rearing matters.

This spousal harmony enables the family to rally in the face of daily or catastrophic crisis. Wilson also provides a list of crisis management tools which can be used for self-evaluation:

1. *The responsible parties have a realistic perception of the event.*

Parents can determine the significance of the negative event and can rally themselves to respond. They can tolerate tension if the stress isn't immediately alleviated. They can endure anxiety if the outcome continues to be unknown, and they can postpone ease if immediate relief is not on the way. These are all healthy coping skills needed by every couple and family unit.

2. *They have developed a support network.*

In the face of losing a geographically close, extended family due to the high mobility of our population, wise adults begin to establish a web of friends, neighborhood relationships, small church groups, and caring acquaintances against the day when disasters strike.

Wilson says the most vulnerable individuals in the future will be those from broken homes who were reared without an extended care network; who have reached maturation in a situation where one parent has carried the financial and emotional burden of work and family life; and who have grown up in an environment where healthy coping mechanisms were not modeled—all this in addition to the emotional scars of rejection.

3. *They have the ability to mobilize resources for stress resolution.*

Wilson maintains that one does not learn crisis strategy without having seen it modeled; modeling by parents is of critical importance to children. We learn stress management by watching and being part of a nucleus of humans who are managing stress.

4. *They possess a meaningful ability to anticipate the future and reorganize to face it.*

Wilson writes, "Confident anticipation of the future can only take place if a person or a family has a philosophy to live by which embodies hope as one of its primary tenets. Hope arises out of a cosmology that asserts all of mankind has a right to life, and that the God who created this universe has provided a system that fosters life."[5]

In fact, when families in a recent study were asked what advice they would give to other families facing crisis, they most frequently responded that prayer and faith in God provide the necessary undergirding to cope.

Does any of this sound familiar to you? Do you see these traits of healthy family crisis management at work in your own home?

NOTES

1. G. Rekers, ed., *Family Building: Six Qualities of a Strong Family* (Ventura, Calif.: Regal Books, 1985), pp. 35-45.
2. J. Jackson, "The Adjustment of the Family to Alcoholism," *Family Living* 18 (1956):361-369.
3. W. P. Wilson, *The Family and Crisis*, report for the Department of Psychiatry, Duke University Medical Center, Durham. N.C.
4. J. I. Kleimann, "Optimal and Normal Family Functioning," *American Journal of Family Therapy*, 1981, pp. 37-44.
5. Wilson, *The Family and Crisis*.

Couples' Discussion Questions

Measure yourselves by Dr. Wilson's criteria of family well-being. Ask yourselves, "How did we cope with the last crisis?"

Did we have a realistic perception of the event?

Did we have an adequate support structure?

Did we mobilize our resources for stress resolution?

Do we anticipate the future and reorganize to face it?

Next, conduct a non-defensive investigation into how you, as a couple, measure against Dr. Stinnett's six criteria for family well-being. Pat yourselves on the back in the areas where you feel you are doing well. Pray together for ideas and help in the areas where you need improvement.

1. Do we have good communication?
2. Do we spend time together?
3. Do we encourage and affirm one another?
4. Do we deal positively with a crisis?
5. Do we have a commitment to the family?
6. Do we have a religious orientation?

If you take the examination and do well, you've got something to crow about. So what if no one says you're doing a good job of parenting? You now have the means to hold up your performance against firmly established measurements of family well-being.

These tools can speak to your own private, personal soul: "Well done! You are doing a good job!"

19
Dialogues:
How Can We Encourage Our Children's Spiritual Growth?

These dialogues, like those in the first half of the book, are intended to stimulate helpful thinking aimed at raising the spiritual temperature of your home.

One way to use these dialogues is for husband and wife to read them to each other. We suggest the husband read David's lines and the wife read Karen's. At those points where either of you have questions or where a helpful observation might be made, stop your reading and discuss together how the material might assist the spiritual development of your home. Then continue reading after you're through discussing that point.

Happy discussions!

Giving Love Is like a Game of Pit

DAVID: Karen, you're notorious in our family for not enjoying games.

KAREN: You mean table games? I admit it: I'd rather read a good book any day or have an interesting conversation than play Monopoly or cards. That bores me; I can't work up a competitive edge, and I usually lose anyway. I do like Pit, though.

DAVID: Isn't that the game based on the commodity exchange where buyers and sellers meet each other in the pit and raucously exchange their bids? Why do you like that game above the others?

KAREN: I'm not sure. For one thing, it's provided our family with a lot of laughs. It also reminds me of the love systems in human nature.

DAVID: You'd better explain that.

KAREN: Well, each individual has a personal way to measure the giving of love. One person might measure love by gifts on special days, birthdays, and anniversaries. This person may have a tendency to be hurt when his own birthday is forgotten. Think for a moment. How do you know when people love you? How do you personally measure love? How do you trade, give, and receive love?

DAVID: Oh, when people do nice things for me.

KAREN: No, no! Be specific: For example, I know you measure love when I jump in and wholeheartedly support your plans, your dreams, your world-changing projects. You believe people love you when they work alongside you, when they pull behind you, when they are interested in the development of your latest scheme. Am I right?

DAVID: Yes, you probably are. How do you measure love?

KAREN: Well, I measure your love for me when you give me free, unplotted, unscheduled, spontaneous time . . .

DAVID: . . . and you married a compulsive workaholic . . .

KAREN: . . . and you married an undisciplined, free- spirited, artistic type. Each of us has a different, private exchange we use to measure love.

DAVID: Now I see. In Pit you want to accumulate one particular commodity; it's hard to get excited over anything else. You're saying that love is the same. If we misunderstand the way one another measures love, it's a little like getting barley when corn is what you really wanted.

KAREN: You got it! Hasn't learning to cope with this difference in our private love exchanges been one of the biggest adjustments in our marriage? If I told you that I'd set a whole day aside as a gift for you, you'd probably say, "Great! Let's get that two-week project planned. We'll be way ahead of schedule, so we'll be free to work on that book manuscript that's due."

DAVID: And if I said I had set a whole day aside as a gift for you, you'd say, "Great! Let's go see the special exhibit at the Art Institute, have lunch downtown, and roam around some ethnic shops."

KAREN: Sounds wonderful! At least we're developing an idea of what we can give each other so that love is known and received on an appropriate emotional level. We're no longer trading in unequal exchanges—getting two barleys when we wanted two ryes. Not understanding this concept of the love exchange is a basic area of pain in marriages, in in-law relationships, between parents and their children, and in friendships.

DAVID: That's why when some people choose a gift that means love to them, the person receiving it shows little enthusiasm. We need to ask ourselves, "What is this person's love commodity? Does he or she trade in oats or wheat?"

KAREN: Right. Often, someone gives clues about their love exchange by what they give us. Or, what's wrong with coming right out and asking, "What special things do people do for you that give you the greatest feeling of love? What kind of gifts give you the most pleasure?"

DAVID: It's interesting to note that when God wanted to communicate his love for the world, he gave that which was most precious to him—his own son. "Greater love has no man than this, that a man lay down his life for his friends," said Christ. In God's mind, that sacrificial act of giving was the ultimate measurement of love.

KAREN: Interestingly enough, when we ask ourselves, "How will God know that I love him?" we can safely assume that his love exchange, the way he measures our love for him, is the degree of totality by which we give ourselves to him.

DAVID: That's a terrific thought. I wonder if we should get that unicycle for the child whose birthday is coming soon? I was thinking a twenty-five volume set of the complete works of Mark Twain would be especially nice.

KAREN: I think you're trying to trade in wheat and that kid wants oats. This is one game I know how to play!

Teaching Kids the Art of Communication

DAVID: American adults spend an average of forty-four hours per week watching television. Some of the appalling fallout from that fact is that we are fast losing the ability to make decent and interesting conversation. Have you noticed this?

KAREN: You're right, David. It's rare to find people with the ability to talk intelligently about a wide range of topics. I had a five-hour delay at the Denver airport recently and a young man who was also waiting for an airplane to Chicago overwhelmed me with his ability to talk about literature, philosophy, current issues. He was twenty-four years old and his good mind definitely helped redeem that unwanted five-hour delay. But this kind of encounter is rare; I came home thinking how conversationally inadequate many Americans really are.

DAVID: Our children often complain that their friends can't talk about anything but what they've seen on television that week, or which movie they liked or didn't like. Acting as a chauffeur one night for the children taught me the truth of their complaint. The conversation of the youngsters sitting in the back seat focused exclusively on the TV shows they'd watched or missed the night before.

KAREN: Not to mention the intellectual, cultural, and spiritual impoverishment it represents, this is particularly sad because the art of good conversation requires only two basic abilities: the ability to ask good questions and the ability to listen.

DAVID: At any rate, I'm glad we're determined not only to learn to be good conversationalists ourselves, but to teach our children how to hold their own with the good conversationalists of the world . . .

KAREN: . . . as well as with the not-so-good conversationalists.

DAVID: We do this with a family game we've devised.

KAREN: Many different people sit around our dinner table— friends of the family, Christian leaders, people from our church, guests who are interviewed on our radio broadcast. We use this as a time to play our conversational game.

DAVID: There are two rules to the game. Number one: Each family member is allowed to ask the special guest two questions. Number two: The special guest must answer each question as honestly as possible.

KAREN: The children ask questions like, "If you had all the money you needed and a week to go anywhere you wanted to go, where would you go?" "What is the best book you ever read?" "When did you become a Christian?" "Who was a girl (or fellow) you liked when you were in junior high?"

DAVID: The questions can't become stock because invariably someone will steal your favorite question. Then you're forced to become original. So we witness a great variety in the family questions.

KAREN: Not only does this game provide us with wonderful family dinner times, but it also makes our guests feel special; they realize we really want to know them personally. It also demonstrates our belief that children are an important part of table conversation.

DAVID: Most importantly, it gave our children, from grade school age through junior high to high school to college, the secure ability to relate to strangers, to people in different social and economic classes, to folks from other cultures and faiths. All they have to do is ask questions and really listen.

KAREN: That's the basis for all conversational arts. The more we ask, the more we learn; the more we listen, the more we know. And the more our interest is piqued to learn, the more questions we'll ask. I can't count how many times I've watched the children make their way conversationally in unusual and potentially awkward social situations. And I can't count how many times someone in our family has said, "I had the most interesting conversation recently."

DAVID: Actually, our model for this is not just a social model; it's basically a spiritual one. Christ was the great Question Asker. He asked, "Can the wedding guests mourn as long as the bridegroom is with them?" and "Do you believe that I am able to do this?" He answered challengers' questions with other questions. "What did you go out into the wilderness to see?" he asked the crowd regarding John the Baptist. In fact, a fascinating Bible study would be to survey the Gospels regarding the questions Jesus asked.

KAREN: But he asked all these questions in order to get to the spiritual heart of the matter. Many men and women are never the same when they truthfully respond to the questions of Christ.

DAVID: And that is the deep-seated reason for our conversational family game: It gives us and our children the comfortable ability to ask questions of strangers and friends and to listen deeply as we gradually move closer to the spiritual heart of things.

KAREN: And that has to be the truest art of conversation anyone can learn!

You Mean You Don't Have a TV?!

KAREN: While speaking to a group of about five hundred people recently, I casually mentioned that we hadn't had a television in our home for nearly thirteen years. The rest of my speech was interrupted by a prolonged ovation.

DAVID: I think that response indicates that, whereas many parents aren't ready to take the drastic action of total withdrawal, they are nevertheless looking for some ideas on how to tame the tube.

KAREN: A.C. Nielsen reports that children under five watch an average of 23.5 hours of TV a week. That's almost one day out of seven!

DAVID: And adult viewing is much higher. According to Nielsen again, the average adult watches about forty-four hours of television a week. Apart from sleeping, this is the biggest block of time spent by an individual in any area of daily living!

KAREN: Television is definitely an influencer. After intensive research study, many sociologists and psychologists identify TV as the primary influence in shaping youths' emerging adult personalities.

DAVID: In one study, 75 percent of young children's conversations concerned TV events and heroes, and 50 percent of their active play directly imitated recently viewed TV programs.

KAREN: In almost one decade, the main education of the preschool child has passed from the mother's hands to television. George Gerbner, University of Pennsylvania research professor, declares, "The socialization of children has been transferred from parents to TV programmers who are unelected, unnamed, and who are not subject to collective review."

So apart from ditching the set in the alley for garbage pickup, how does an average family tame the tube?

DAVID: The goal we are attempting to achieve is control. We must learn to master the television. It must become our servant, not vice versa.

KAREN: One of the children *did* drop our portable television set, and instead of having it fixed, we *did* toss it in the garbage. Then, after seven years of abstinence, we decided to try it again, but this time with controls. I had concluded that if I didn't monitor TV viewing habits, I was a neglectful parent. So we came to a family consensus that seven hours of TV viewing per week per person was the limit . . .

DAVID: . . . with special dispensations provided for worthwhile TV specials.

KAREN: Right. Part of our TV attack plan was a viewing chart placed beside the set which we all had to check. There was no after-school television viewing, no TV watching unless homework, chores, and practicing was done. Shows watched had to pass a family approval code.

DAVID: And none of us were allowed to switch on the TV just to see what was on. This was a key rule. We tried to stress to the children that they were to review a TV guide for the week ahead and plan their viewing. Those thirty seconds of just seeing what is on can hook a child or an adult for the next two hours.

KAREN: Basically, we felt good about this plan. The only difficulty was that with four children of varying ages, monitoring required a great deal of my energy. And even with the home TV policewoman on the beat, the set was on a great deal!

DAVID: So when the set was stolen in a home burglary, we took that as an obvious word from the Lord and decided to go TV cold turkey again.

KAREN: What a relief! It is so wonderful not to have to contend with this intrusive element. I think every family should experiment with at least a month or a season of television fasting.

DAVID: People frequently ask how our children felt about this, so I regularly polled them to find out. Invariably, they all voted "no" to getting a television set. Often, after having visited a friend's home or after having watched television in a motel as we traveled, they would make the unsolicited comment, "We're so glad we don't have a TV!"

KAREN: Living without a television has meant we've had to put extra effort into making sure the children were informed, well-read, and exposed to the best theater, the best arts our culture has to offer. But I much prefer this intentional, participatory type of learning to the passive viewing which predominates in so many families.

DAVID: Without TV, we have seven extra hours each week . . .

KAREN: . . . sometimes six people times seven extra hours per week . . .

DAVID: . . . to devote to communication within the family, to attend a special event together, to develop personal interests, to read, to think. Psalm 101 says, "I will walk in my house with blameless heart. I will set before my eyes no vile thing."

KAREN: Others may not want to dump the TV as we did . . .

DAVID: . . . but for the sake of the family, they must at least learn to tame it.

The Advantages and Disadvantages of Halos

DAVID: Have you ever thought how different our lives would be if we had halos?

KAREN: You mean if we actually had rings of light behind our heads to indicate saintliness?

DAVID: Yep! A true measurement of spirituality. I can think of some obvious advantages to having halos. Imagine attending a church board meeting where there is disagreement regarding your opinion. You could just bend your head slightly . . .

KAREN: Tip the halo, you mean?

DAVID: That would silence everyone.

KAREN: I think I'm getting your idea. But suppose you were in a traffic jam where you lost your cool and started to honk your horn? Or suppose you were in a grocery store and you were starting to steam because your kids were swiping stuff off the shelves? Your halo would immediately tell everyone around that you weren't acting very saintly.

DAVID: Now that's a disadvantage. You might need to carry around a big hat to cover it at awkward moments. But then, think how great it would be if you got lost in the woods while on a camping trip with your kids or how convenient if you needed something in a dark closet.

KAREN: But!—If there was persecution of the church and the body of Christ had to go underground, halo headgear might lead to decapitation.

DAVID: Another disadvantage. A real advantage, though, would be knowing where one another was spiritually.

It would take away the guesswork. If a halo shone very brightly, you would know its wearer was deeply spiritual. If it was flashing off and on, or just flickering, you would know that that person needed to get his or her spiritual act together.

KAREN: If we had halos, would the old saintly qualities still apply?

DAVID: Austrian theologian Adolph Hull believed that "the essentials the church saw in saints have not altered. A saint must exhibit a heroic degree of virtue . . . his works must be out of the ordinary. The life of a saint should display a certain personal serenity."

KAREN: That's good. I'd hate to throw away such things as purity, goodness, self-control, etc. But then, aren't all believers saints?

DAVID: Yes, Scripture teaches that we are all saints together in the body of Christ. But there are those unique people who are especially saintly.

KAREN: The definition I like most describes a saint as a "window through which another world is glimpsed, a person through whom the light of God shines."

DAVID: Artists have tried to visualize these qualities with a ring of light—a halo. Let's put together a list of qualities that define visible saintliness, or exceptional spirituality. One would have to be personal holiness, the kind of virtuous person who characteristically demonstrates victory over sin.

KAREN: Another characteristic comes from the word *sanctification,* which is used in Scripture to describe a saint. It means "to be set aside on God's behalf." That involves self- denial, self-sacrifice, and a desire to please God.

DAVID: A third quality often associated with saints is humility or lowliness. These people don't strive for the spotlight. They are satisfied with doing their good deeds anonymously. Also, a saint might possess a personal serenity. By that I mean a sense of calm, of peace, all gained from a life of prayer.

KAREN: I think of serenity as the quality of life that leaves one unbattered in the midst of battering circumstances. These people carry tremendous responsibilities but have learned not to become nervous or upset.

DAVID: And perhaps their underlying characteristic is a life of unusual love. Their love of God is often so great it motivates them to sacrifice themselves for others.

KAREN: Of course, Jesus is the supreme example of saintliness. Yet, these characteristics are measurable on a marital and a family level, too. Is our life together characterized by a growing degree of personal holiness? Are we setting ourselves aside for God's use? Can we detect developing humility, serenity, and a life of love for each other?

DAVID: All of us should strive for these qualities. Ephesians 4:1-3 states, "As a prisoner for the Lord, then, I urge you to live a life worthy of the calling you have received. Be completely humble and gentle; be patient, bearing with one another in love. Make every effort to keep the unity of the Spirit through the bond of peace."

KAREN: Do you think Christian parents should be raising a bunch of saints, all of them running around with shining halos?

DAVID: Well, I can think of some advantages—parents wouldn't have to purchase night lights for those little ones afraid of the dark.

KAREN: The greatest advantage, however, of raising a family whose lives together demonstrate the qualities of saintliness, is that worldly-oriented families would see God's light shining through the windows of the average Christian home.

DAVID: We need to ask ourselves if our family is

learning to develop these qualities. And what do we have to do to develop them more?

KAREN: Then we need to learn to say to one another: "Hey! Great! Your halo is showing!"

Karen

Epilogue

Throughout the centuries, pilgrims have commented on the peculiar quality of the light of Jerusalem. Situated seven miles outside the city in the Judean hills is a synagogue attached to the Hadassah-Hebrew University Medical Center. Its twelve gorgeous stained-glass windows capture the particular quality and radiance of that famous light.

The artist who created these exquisite windows was Marc Chagall, perhaps the greatest Jewish artist of our time.

David and I saw these windows on our first trip to Israel in 1978. I remember sitting within the synagogue, stunned by the iridescence of the light as it shone though the glass designs. Three windows to a wall, each one representing a tribe of Israel, eleven feet high and eight feet wide, radiating shafts of jeweled color onto the stone floor below, and onto me as I lifted my head.

For centuries the artist with religious sensibilities has attempted to capture visually the inner spiritual experience. Many paintings of old could have been titled: "Holy Light on Common Things." Long ago, the sacred artist knew that he must keep himself pure so that his work would be pure, not only so that the viewer could see with physical eyes what had been painted, but also with inner eyes suddenly opened to spiritual truth.

This centuries-old quest of the religious artist reaches a culmination of sorts in the twelve glowing windows of Marc Chagall in the Judean hillside. There they illumine the exquisite light; there religious symbols of the Old Testament are magnified by the shining day; and there the viewer, a spiritual pilgrim, stands within the very work of art, lifts her head, and is stunned.

Why is any of this important in a book on spiritual life in the home? It's because I believe that each man and woman has the potential to become the living artwork though which the light of God can shine.

Look at this analogy any way you like. You might say, "I'm the artist who will show forth God's light in the world."

I believe this. Each of us can be an artisan in the way we create a home, in the way we form a marriage, in the way we conduct our daily work or rear a child or sing a song or live fully in each moment of each day. When done well, these are works of art.

Or look at the analogy this way. You (or your marriage or your family) are the window, and the pieces of your life are the stained glass—dark and uninteresting, without pattern, until the morning breaks and the sun rises and the light glimmers. Suddenly a viewer, looking at you, sees that the pieces make a pattern and the colors of yourself are dazzling and rich.

How does this happen, this recreation of the common into the uncommon? How is the simple craft transformed into a living work of art?

We become God's living work of art in the world by putting ourselves in the way of his light and letting him shine through us. If we want to be windows of God's light to the other members of our family, we must put ourselves in the light's way and *stay there*. We must work hard at our own spirituality.

Unfortunately, we suspect many Christians are unconvinced that spirituality is worth the effort. As Americans we strive for economic achievement, for professional advancement, for material accumulation, for educational status; but the one quality that is worth acquiring above all these others, whose absence makes all these others meaningless, is a lively spiritual life.

Our spiritual development, all too often, comes after the forty-four hours (on an average) of adult television viewing per week. It comes after the half-hour in the newspaper. It comes after the three-mile run and the aerobics class, after vacations, after a sixty-hour work week.

In short, our priorities say and our activities shout that we do not believe that working at spirituality in our homes is worth it.

The situation will remain as it is until we become convinced that there is nothing greater that we can achieve, nothing more significant to which we can hold each other accountable, nothing more profound that we can give to one another, to our children, and ultimately to our society, than spiritual development.

Yes, spirituality *is* ephemeral, elusive, hard to define. Honest, sincere people are confused as to what it is.

When we were in the pastorate and in the process of choosing church elders, we emphasized that the appointees needed to be spiritual people. Some in our young congregation considered this a point of unfair discrimination. One man voiced what was perhaps a question of others:

"What do you mean, you need *spiritual* candidates? We're all Christians, aren't we? Aren't we *all* spiritual?"

What is spirituality? Is it regular family devotions? Is it church attendance? Is it reading the Scriptures every day? Is it refraining from certain activities and adhering to certain codes?

Spirituality, as hard as it is to define, is a desperately longed-for quality. We want to see it in our religious leaders. We want pastors and Bible teachers to be men and women of God. Spouses wish it of each other. We mourn the fact that some of our fathers were mere Christian functionaries rather than men of faith. If only we had some models, we think, perhaps then we would know what spirituality looks like, and we could copy it.

How can we touch spirituality? How can we take it into our grasp and finger it? We need form, substance, a model, something hard to bump up against, something to feel so that the frustratingly unseen becomes real.

Spiritual leadership in our home is very far from perfect, but it's tangible. It is seeable. It is pillows stacked on the living room sofa where someone prayed late last night. It is the backside of a man in his study bending into the dim light over his study table. It is a wife's Bible so used that the pages are soft, the binding malleable. It is a mind so disciplined through the years by habitual considerations that its first questions now are, "What would Christ say? What does God think? How would the Lord act?"

Spirituality can be heard in our home.

Spiritual leadership is a couple who love worship, who call a family together on Saturday evening to ready their hearts for tomorrow's praise. It is the verbal reminder: "Come home early. Tomorrow is Sunday." It is the familiar question we tease and joke about but would feel neglected if David never asked: "How are you doing spiritually?" It's the wonderful welcome when friends come to visit.

Spirituality has physical form.

It is barging into a room and finding a wife and mother on her knees. It is the crease marks on the forehead of a man after he has pressed it to the bed in extended prayer.

Spiritual leadership is a one-to-one accountability Bible study on Amos with the oldest teenager. It's bedtime with the ten-year-old and a heavy discussion about a playmate who has been influenced to change his reading material from pornographic magazines to Christian comics. It's cards with Bible memory verses. It's reading a story by Flannery O'Connor out loud and laughing at her version of humanity and discussing the action of grace in her tale.

Spiritual leadership is a man on Saturday, with the house full of wife, four children, two dogs, one pregnant cat, guests and extended family, desperately hunting for a quiet place to fulfill a weekly prayer vow.

Spiritual leadership is a man or a woman, sometimes exasperatingly human, who nevertheless give the spiritual life material meaning. In our home, spirituality has by no means reached perfection—but it is tangible, it can be seen, heard, experienced, and known.

Spiritual people are God's living work of art in the world, his stained-glass windows. He shines through us when we put ourselves in the way of his light.

It is as simple and as difficult as that.

If we are to maintain physical shapeliness, we know we will have to go on an adequate diet, stick with it, and commit ourselves to an exercise program for the rest of our lives. Merely living in a health-conscious family is no guarantee of physical fitness.

It is no different in the spiritual realm. Living in a

spiritually-conscious family is no guarantee of spiritual fitness. The spiritual life must be *done*.

We must place ourselves in a church that stimulates our growth and challenges our lethargy. We must read the Bible, pray, and obey what we learn. We must exercise spirituality each day as much as possible and we must commit ourselves to it for the rest of our lives.

A recent bestseller had an intriguing title: *The Man Who Mistook His Wife for a Hat*. The title story concerns a musician of distinction who learned to live with an acute form of visual agnosia, a disorder of recognition. He literally reached for his wife and attempted to place her on his head as one would a hat.

The author, neurologist Dr. Oliver Sacks, later tells the story of Jimmy G., a middle-aged man whose memory retained only those events prior to 1945. Jimmy thought he was twenty instead of forty-nine and could not remember events which had happened two minutes before or conversations seconds before. Jimmy suffered from a neurological disorder called Korsakov's syndrome.

"Jimmy is a man isolated in a single moment of being with a moat of forgetting all around him," Sacks wrote in his notes. "He is a man without a past or future, stuck in a constantly changing, meaningless moment."

Finally, in one frustrated exchange, the neurologist turned to the nurses in the Catholic hospital in which he was working and asked, "Do you think he has a soul?" The nurses were outraged by his question and replied, "Watch Jimmy in chapel and judge for yourself."

Sacks did just that:

> I was moved, profoundly moved and impressed, because I saw here an intensity and steadiness of attention and concentration that I had never seen before in him or conceived him capable of. I watched him kneel and take

> the Sacrament on his tongue, and could not doubt the fullness and totality of Communion, the perfect alignment of his spirit with the spirit of the Mass. . . . There was no forgetting, no Korsakov's then . . . for he was no longer at the mercy of a faulty and fallible mechanism—that of meaningless sequences and memory traces . . . but was absorbed in an act, an act of his whole being. . . . Clearly Jimmy found himself, found continuity and reality, in the absoluteness of spiritual attention and act. The Sisters were right—he did find his soul here.

Then this scientist concludes his remarkable story about Jimmy, the man without memory, by stating:

> I have known Jimmy now for nine years—and neuropsychologically, he has not changed in the least. He still has the severest, most devastating Korsakov's, cannot remember isolated items for more than a few seconds. . . . But humanly, spiritually, he is at times a different man altogether—no longer fluttering, restless, bored, and lost but deeply attentive to the soul of the world. . . . Empirical science takes no account of the soul. Perhaps there is a philosophical as well as a clinical lesson here; that in Korsakov's or dementia, or other such catastrophes, however great the organic damage and dissolution, there remains the undiminished possibility of reintegration by art, by communion, by touching the spirit; and this can be preserved in what seems at first a hopeless state of neurological devastation.[1]

The story grips me, because I seem forever to be in the process of finding (and keeping) my own soul. My frailty demands constant surveillance. The joint ministries of David and Karen Mains always have a constant, underlying theme, this reminder to other Christians: *Remember your soul.*

How can a Christian lose his or her soul? Oh, we do it all the time. Minutes, days, weeks, months go by in which we do not consider our souls one whit. Out of sight, out of mind, out of consciousness. And our souls are literally lost to us.

Most of us exhibit a form of Korsakov's in our persistent tendency to forget the spiritual. To prevent this memory loss from becoming permanent, we must commit ourselves as Christian couples—in the midst of busy lives, in the midst of an increasingly depraved society—to find our own souls again, to journey together and then to lead those who are dependent upon us into their own discovery of their souls before God.

The apostle Paul once preached a sermon in which he said,

> The God who made the world and everything in it is the Lord of heaven and earth and does not live in temples built by hands. And he is not served by human hands, as if he needed anything, because he himself gives all men life and breath and everything else. From one man he made every nation of men, that they should inhabit the whole earth. . . . that men would seek him and perhaps reach out for him and find him, though he is not far from each one of us. For in him we live and move and have our being (Acts 17:24-28).

God is near. The problem is that we forget. We suffer from a spiritual Korsakov's syndrome.

As Christians, we must remember who we are and what our essential obligation is to those who follow us. We must again get in touch with our own souls, find them in order to avoid losing our way in the parade of the world.

In Memphis, Tennessee, women who had invited me to speak at their church retreat gave me a tour of the city.

"Oh, you have to see the Peabody ducks," said one of my new friends as we took the expressway that led downtown. "The Peabody ducks are a Memphis tradition."

A few minutes before 10:30 A.M. we entered the lobby of the Peabody Hotel, a Memphis landmark completely refurbished for the comfort and pleasure of its guests. Dark wood paneling and lovely oriental carpets adorned the grand reception hall where a large travertine marble fountain marked the middle. Huge vases of fresh flowers accented the room and I noticed that a large crowd had begun to gather on either side of a red carpet that stretched from the elevator to the fountain.

Every eye was fixed on the elevator floor marker. Voices grew hushed as it showed the elevator descending from floor twelve, to floor eleven, to floor ten, to floor eight, then finally to the ground floor. The doors opened and a loudspeaker boomed, "Ladies and gentlemen, we want to welcome you to the Peabody Hotel!"

The voice recounted the hotel's history, told of the Peabody family and about the fountain made from one piece of marble. Then it said, "And now we're glad that you've gathered to observe a fifty-year tradition—the parade of the Peabody ducks!"

Music blared out a march tune. Suddenly three mallard ducks, a male and two females, waddled down the red carpet and plunged into the fountain in the middle of the lobby, coached by the duck master.

I learned this event happens twice a day, once when the ducks come down from the duck penthouse on the roof, and once at the end of the day when the duck master takes them back up. On certain holidays it's almost impossible to get in to see this production.

We laughed off and on all day, delighting in this rare event. Later that evening at dinner, the pastor heard us describe our experience and remarked, "It's so absurd, you have to take it seriously!"

My friends, the truth is this: We Christians are on parade before a world of watching eyes, before our children, before our spouses, our extended family, neighbors, and co-workers. We have it within our power to find our souls, to become holy men, women, and families, who command respect because our lives are significantly different from those of the world around us.

Or, if we choose, we can lose our way and join a waddling duck parade—cute as can be, but taken seriously only because we're so absurd.

In fourteenth-century Europe a parade of another kind took place. A fresco in a French church shows Death, a ghoulish skeleton, leading all kinds of people by the hand—cardinal, king, knight, noblewoman, poet, merchant, sergeant, child, doctor, serf, and mother, all from differing social levels. This grisly fresco depicting a medieval play is titled *Danse Macabre*— "Dance of Death."

The point of both the mural and the drama is that "Power, honor, riches are naught. . . ." In other words, consider your end and the life that leads you there. The people portrayed in that mural are co-workers, relatives, friends: "It is yourself," says the inscription under the fresco.

Why this fourteenth-century fascination with death? When you recall that in those days you could meet that grim specter on any corner, it's not hard to understand.

In October 1347, two ships put to shore at the harbor of Messina in Sicily with dead and dying men at the oars. By January 1348, the bubonic plague had penetrated France and by 1350 historians estimate that a third of the world had died. Though no one in truth knows the exact death toll, a third of Europe would have equaled roughly twenty million people. The disease was so lethal that people often went to bed well and died before they woke. Those who lived could not keep up with the burials.

The Black Death returned for the fourth round in 1388-1390, reducing Europe's population by 40 to 50 percent of what it had been when the century opened. So rapidly did it spread that a French physician, Simon de Covino, exclaimed that one sick person "could infect the whole world." A stricken populace said to one another and believed, "This is the end of the world."[2]

You see, death *was* dancing.

When death is dancing in the world, it is not the time for Christians to be misplacing their souls and marching in waddling duck parades.

The twentieth century faces its own dance of death. We live in a world tipping on the edge of nuclear destruction, where drought and starvation roam unchecked in countries whose names we scarcely know, where AIDS has become a lethal, modern equivalent of the Black Plague, threatening to jump the boundaries of the high-risk communities and to infect the innocent as well as the guilty.

How can we settle for being ducks on parade?

We need holy people, holy mothers and fathers, doing holy work, advancing fearlessly in an unholy world.

We need spiritual men and women, holy people whose spirituality can be assessed, known, seen.

We need to commit ourselves to lives of saintliness, to model spirituality in our own homes.

We need to be filled with righteous indignation

about our own faults and the faults of the world.

We need to be filled with godly compassion for those who suffer, believing that prayer is an indispensable ingredient in challenging the strongholds of evil.

We must, together with our families, march to the drumbeat of a different Drummer, Christ.

Paul, in Romans 13:11-14, calls us to this holy parade:

> And do this, understanding the present time. The hour has come for you to wake up from your slumber. . . . let us put aside the deeds of darkness and put on the armor of light. Let us behave decently, as in the daytime, not in orgies and drunkenness, not in sexual immorality and debauchery, not in dissension and jealousy. Rather, clothe yourselves with the Lord Jesus Christ, and do not think about how to gratify the desires of the sinful nature.

I am bothered by Christian duck parades. By the waddling absurdity in fellow Christians. By the breakdown of Christian marriages. I'm shocked when I look into my own soul and discover a tendency to quack.

So in this superficial world, I'm not only determined to find my soul, but for the sake of family and friends and the church, I'm determined to keep it.

God needs men and women whose spirituality permeates their surroundings and communicates itself all around, redemptively working holiness in the world.

Listen very carefully—do you hear what I hear? I hear the stepbeat of another marching order, of those who have put on Christ, the Drumbeater. I hear the far-off cadence of a holy parade. I hear the call, "Awake, O sleeper, arise from the dead, and Christ shall give you light!"

I am determined not to be a duck on parade. And

I am determined, as God gives me strength, that our home will be a way station for all those, friends and children, who march along the Way.

Will you join me?

NOTES

1. Oliver Sacks, *The Man Who Mistook His Wife for a Hat* (New York: Perennial Library, 1987), pp. 37-39.

2. B. W. Tuchman, *A Distant Mirror: The Calamitous 14th Century* (New York: Ballantine Books, 1987), pp. 91-94, 505-510.

Couples' Discussion Questions

Think through these questions alone, in private.

1. What time in your life were you spiritually most sensitive?
2. Do you need to find your soulish self again?
3. In what parade have you been marching? Give it a name.

Then spin some dreams with your spouse. Talk about these discussion questions:

1. If together you could create a spiritual environment in your own home, what would it be like?
2. Of the families you know, which seem to be successfully creating a spiritual environment? Why do you say this? How do you know? What is tangible about these families' spiritual lives?

Appendix 1

Unanswered Questions

This is a book that *doesn't* answer many questions. Some of those questions are ones you may be asking, such as:

1. You have shown how to teach spirituality to your children when their prayers are answered; how do you teach it when their prayers (or your own) *aren't* answered?

2. How do you handle the time demands when your kids are little? There just doesn't seem to be enough time or energy when you're putting together a profession, running after children, establishing a marriage, and becoming a mature adult yourself.

3. It's easy to be creative in teaching spirituality when your kids are teens; but how can you be creative when your children are knee-high (or thereabouts)?

4. How do you find time for spiritual input when your children are involved in school, your professional life is demanding, and you and your spouse are carrying major responsibilities in the community and in the church?

5. How do you find the time for spiritual emphasis when the dinner hour seems to be eaten in shifts around church meetings, sports practices, theater club rehearsals, homework in the library, the master's degree night classes?

6. How do you encourage the spiritual growth of adult children who are no longer in your home? Or how do you encourage the spiritual growth of adult children who have lived on their own and have now returned to live with you?

7. What if you're a single parent? How in the world do you enhance your children's spiritual growth all on your own?

8. You haven't mentioned holding on to a spiritual life when you and your spouse are taking care of sick and aging parents. What about it?

9. What if your spouse is not only passive about spiritual things, but isn't even a Christian?

10. How do you and your spouse hold together when a child dies?

11. What about extended family gatherings where there is no emphasis on spiritual matters? Even religious holidays have no religious emphasis. We would like to change this in our extended family, but just don't know what to do.

12. What about men holding other men accountable for spiritual growth? Did David have any accountability relationship outside of his marriage?

We haven't answered any of these questions or a thousand like them. We haven't (until now) even raised them. Instead, we have described an invaluable tool, the meeting of your Executive Management Team.

When the next imponderable thrusts itself your way, convene your family board. Discuss the issue. Spend time in prayer over it. You will be amazed at how many answers are to be discovered in this executive function. You will be amazed at how many ready solutions are available in the tandem pulling together of a dedicated twosome.

"That's fine for married couples who are in agreement!" someone cries. "But what if spouses are pulling against each other? What if you don't have a spouse?"

Form an ad hoc executive committee. Ask someone who loves you, who is concerned about your present, your future, and your children to meet with you regularly to discuss family concerns. Commit yourselves to positive problem solving and to times of prayer.

Because your spouse is uncooperative (or because you are single) does not mean that the burden-bearing dynamics of Christ's body are unavailable to you. A Christian grandparent, a sister or brother, a friend from your Bible study, a spiritual mentor could all form this ad hoc group with you.

The answers to the questions are near, found in the love and prayers and concern of another. They're not always found easily, but they can be discovered through diligence and patient seeking. You *can* create a spiritual environment in your home. No one need accomplish this monumental task alone.

God is near and so are his people.

Appendix 2

Can Science Confirm the Benefits of Spirituality?

A friend recently asked at a small group meeting, "Has anyone seen any statistics comparing the incidence of psychological health between Christians and non-Christians?"

Good question!

When we look to the carefully controlled research study of the scientific community, we find a dearth of work that factors in religion. In fact, the scientific and psychological communities have built a national health system by virtually ignoring or outright canceling the spiritual factor.

The severity of that denial was highlighted by a group of scientific researchers which reviewed ten years of articles published in the *Journal of Family Practice* (selected because it reflects the current status of clinical practice and research in family medicine). The group discovered that of a total of 1,086 studies from 1976-1986, only twenty-one measured any religious variables.[1]

In another systematic analysis of four major psychiatric journals, some 2,348 articles were reviewed, and only fifty-nine (2.5 percent) included any quantified religious variables.[2] The authors of this report fault the fact that the bulk of clinical psychiatric literature focuses on illness—"a skewed sample without a comparison group"—and maintain that the function of religion in normal lives presents quite a different interpretation. Moreover, they point out that a substantial number of psychotherapists are committed to "religious apostasy" which influences their viewpoints on the value of religion to health and well-being.

In a survey of the American Psychiatric Association membership, 43 percent said they believed in God.[3] Only 5 percent of the membership of the American Psychological Association said they believed in God.[4]

These statistics help to explain the paucity of research on religion. Not only does this deliberate disregard influence knowledge of how spirituality influences health, it denies the fact that spirituality helps form our national identity and it exposes a terribly unrealistic bias in the mental and physical health professions.

The fact is, most Americans have some theistic belief system. From 1944 to 1981, the Gallup Poll interviewed Americans a dozen times about their belief in God and discovered no percentile decline. In 1944, 95 percent believed in God; in 1981, 95 percent believed in God.[5]

Four national surveys over the past ten years (not including popular magazine reader surveys) have documented the substantial religious orientation of the population of the United States. More than 90 percent of those polled believe in God; more than 40 percent attend religious services weekly or more often.[6] And yet opinion-makers, legislators, and the influencers of our culture often call upon "experts" in the health communities for help in interpreting policies that affect the life of our nation's families.

Psychiatric researcher David B. Larson and his collaborators further point out that even when religious factors are included in scientific research, religiosity tends to be measured by an unsatisfactory determinant—denominational alliance—rather than by a more definitive measurement. Religion is a dynamic, multi- faceted entity. Commitment to it can hardly be determined by whether one is a Baptist or a Catholic.

Sociological researchers do not make the same mistake. They employ sophisticated religious variables which include frequency of Bible study, prayer, church attendance, etc. The Larson research team questions its professional health colleagues and asks: "Why does psychiatric research so infrequently consider religious variables, and when it does, why is the methodology so inadequate?"[7]

Why indeed? And why this lengthy discussion on psychological research in a book discussing the importance of spirituality in the Christian family?

One reason is that research forms the opinions and concepts of the way Americans view themselves.

Another reason is that the limited amount of health research that factors in religiosity (using sophisticated methods of determinants) *indicates that religious people are benefiting from their belief system*. In other words, these studies, though limited numerically, are saying, "It's healthy to be actively religious."

The Personal Benefits of Religion

A number of studies suggest that people who are actively involved in their religion may experience decreased morbidity in a variety of areas. Mormons, for instance, have been shown to have relatively low cancer rates, which presumably may be related to abstinence from tobacco, alcohol, and caffeine.[8]

A study of health center patients in Glasgow found that those who participated actively in their religion reported fewer physical symptoms than religious nonparticipants.[9] Another study noted that blood pressure was lower among church-attenders than among nonattenders.[10] Patients with rectal cancer were less likely to be religiously active than religiously active control groups.[11] Another study found a consistent pattern of lower systolic and diastolic blood pressures among frequent church attenders compared with that of infrequent attenders, independent of age, obesity, cigarette smoking, or socio-economic status.[12]

Four other studies have reported associations of religious activity with decreased mortality rates.

One study found an almost two times greater mortality risk for both men and women who were infrequent church attenders, compared with those who attended church weekly or more often.[13]

Another study followed approximately 2,700 persons over eight to ten years in the Tecumseh Community Health Study and found that regular church attendance was associated with lower mortality rates for women (not for men), after controlling for other appropriate cardiovascular risk factors.[14]

Yet another study among elderly people discovered that the non-religiously active had mortality levels twice those of their religiously active counterparts, controlling for age, education, income, race, sex, health, and previous hospitalizations.[15]

Admittedly, research on how an active religious life affects physical health is scarce. But the early, credible samplings (excluding those with unsophisticated levels of religious measurements) are certainly intriguing.

Religious commitment or practices have been shown to affect emotional health. Studies show positive associations between high levels of religious commitment and mental health, between religious activity and life satisfaction, between church attendance and diminished suicide risk, between church attendance and diminished psychiatric illness.[16]

These indicators persuade us to conclude that there seem to be tangible measurements, both physical and psychological, that say it is worth working to establish a spiritual environment in the Christian family.

The Longing for Spirituality

The data on spirituality doesn't stop here. Recently and strangely (in light of popular media denigration of Christianity), a longing for spirituality seems to have broken out into the general public. Polls have shown that spirituality is important to larger numbers of Americans than our information society ever suspected.

Glamour magazine conducted a survey titled "What Are Your Personal Feelings on Religion?"[17] The results indicated a powerful swing to life's spiritual side. The reporter, Lisa Schwarzbaum, noted the surprising swell in interest but interpreted the poll like this: "The fact of a return to faith isn't the only news. For women, the *nature* of faith and religious belief has changed. Religion now often merges old traditions with new attitudes to form beliefs and practices that are individualistic and self-styled to fit women's needs and desires."

Given the readership profile of a style-conscious magazine such as *Glamour*—according to *Writer's Market*, "contemporary, featuring fashion, beauty, decorating, travel, food and entertainment, current mores"—we personally think the results are astounding. Granted, these statistics may reflect movement toward New Age thinking, or toward vague and often undefined religious allegiances, but they nevertheless reveal a hunger for spiritual meaning which belies usual estimates of American interest.

Some 87 percent of the survey's respondents believed that God is always helping them or has helped them through a particular time. Some 80 percent were as religious or more so than they were five years before. Some 79 percent read the Bible; 77 percent prayed at home and/or in a church or synagogue; 54 percent attended church or synagogue regularly, 20 percent attended occasionally. For some 72 percent, religion was a source of inner strength; for 70 percent, it gave a perspective on the important things in life; 64 percent felt religion offered moral and ethical guidance; and 63 percent found it to be a source of spiritual peace.

Only 8 percent responded that religion does not keep pace with the needs of modern women and had no place in life.

The results of *Glamour's* survey aren't isolated or flukish. A *Better Homes and Gardens* survey that asked its middle-level American readership, "Are American Families Finding New Strength in Spirituality?" turned up some familiar-sounding answers.[18] Religion and spirituality are vitally important, these readers said.

Some 76 percent said they relied often on their faith for guidance in everyday family matters; 74 percent said it was very important to share a common faith commitment with their spouses. Some 71 percent felt it was important for children to share their beliefs. Nearly all (91 percent) reported they believed in God; 80 percent believed in a personal God; 87 percent believed in heaven; 76 percent believed in hell; and 89 percent believed in eternal life. Interestingly, some 40 percent felt they were more spiritual or religious than their parents had been.

Though the results might have been skewed by the likelihood that religious people would be more inclined to respond to such a voluntary survey, nevertheless the results were fascinating. Some eighty thousand people responded, and 10,400 clipped a note or a letter of explanation to the survey. Many indicated it was the fact of being a parent that persuaded them to seriously seek answers in religious faith. We close with some of their comments:

"When one becomes a parent, the necessity to provide an ethical framework based on traditional values for one's children becomes a priority."

"I was content to explore my own spiritual and religious needs and beliefs at a relaxed pace until I took on the job of modeling life for two little people."

"I find it interesting that religion seems to be becoming more important in the lives of many of my friends and associates, particularly after they have started families. Though my husband and I were both raised in religious families, we discuss our beliefs much more openly with our children than our parents did with us. I feel it is *essential* for my daughters to have this background."

"My husband and I just started attending church a few months ago. After two years of marriage we felt something was missing in our lives. Religion seems to have been that missing factor. Since we started to attend a local church we've gained new insight. We are both reading the Bible for the first time and enjoying it."

NOTES

1. F. C. Craigie, I. Y. Liu, P. B. Larson, "A Systematic Analysis of Religious Variables in the *Journal of Family Practice*," private research documents.
2. D. B. Larson, E. M. Pattison, D. G. Blazer, A.R. Omran, B. H. Kaplan, "Systematic Analysis of Research on Religious Varibles in Four Major Psychiatric

Journals, 1978-1982," *American Journal of Psychiatry* 143 (March 1986):3.

3. A. N. Franzblau, "Psychiatrists' Viewpoints on Religion and Their Services to Religious Institutions and the Ministry," Task Force Report Number 10, Washington D.C., American Psychiatric Association, 1975.

4. C. P. Ragan, N. H. Malony, B. Beit-Hallahmi, "Psychologists and Religion: Professional Factors Related to Personal Religiosity," paper presented at the Annual Meeting of the American Psychological Association, Washington D.C., September 1976.

5. G. Gallup, *Religion in America: 50 Years, 1935-1985,* Gallup Report 236, May 1985.

6. *The Connecticut Mutual Life Report on American Values in the Eighties* (Hartford: Connecticut Mutual Life Insurance Co., 1981); J. Verhoff, E. Douvan, R. Kulka, *The Inner American* (New York: Basic Books, 1981); C. K. Hadaway, "Life Satisfaction and Religion: A Re-analysis," *Social Forces* 57 (1978): 634-635; Gallup, op. cit.

7. D. B. Larson, E. M. Pattison, D. G. Blazer et al., "The Measurement of Religion in Psychiatric Research," *Psychiatry and Religion: Overlapping Concerns* (Washington D.C.: American Psychiatric Press, 1986).

8. J. L. Lyon, M. R. Klauber, J. W. W. Gardner et al., "Cancer Incidence in Mormons and non-Mormons in Utah, 1966-1970," *New England Journal of Medicine* 294 (1976): 129-133.

9. D. R. Hannay, "Religion and Health," *Social Science and Medicine* 14A (1980): 638-685.

10. A. Walsh, "The Prophylactic Effect of Religion on Blood Pressure Levels Among a Sample of Immigrants," *Social Science and Medicine* 14B (1980):59-63.

11. M. Monk, A. Lilienfield, A. Mendeloff, *Preliminary Report of an Epidemiologic Study of Cancers of the Colon and Rectum*, paper presented at the meeting of the Epidemiology Section of the American Public Health Association, 1962.

12. T. W. Graham, B. H. Kaplan, J. C. Cornoni-Huntley et al,. "Frequency of Church Attendance and Blood Pressure Elevation," *Journal of Behavioral Medicine* 1 (1978);37-43.

13. G. W. Comstock, K. B. Partridge, "Church Attendance and Health," *Journal of Chronic Disease* 25 (1972):665-672.

14. J. S. House, C. Robbins, H. L. Metzner, "The Association of Social Relationships and Activities with Morality: Prospective Evidence from the Tecumseh Community Health Study," *American Journal of Epidemiology* 119 (1984): 129

15. D. M. Zuckerman, S. V. Kasl, A. M. Ostfeld, "Psychosocial Predictors of Mortality Among the Elderly Poor," *American Journal of Epidemiology* 119 (1984):410-423.

16. F. C. Craigie, I. Y. Liu, D. B. Larson, op. cit.

17. *Glamour Magazine*, January 1988, pp. 299-303.

18. *Better Homes and Gardens*, January 1988, pp. 16-27.